Strategic Studies Institute Monograph

LESSONS OF THE IRAQI DE-BA'ATHIFICATION PROGRAM FOR IRAQ'S FUTURE AND THE ARAB REVOLUTIONS

W. Andrew Terrill

May 2012

*****

Comments pertaining to this report are invited and should be forwarded to: Director, Strategic Studies Institute, U.S. Army War College, 45 Ashburn Drive, Bldg. 47, Carlisle, PA 17013-5046.

*****

I would like to thank Dr. Steven Metz and Mary J. Pelusi for useful and insightful comments on earlier drafts of this monograph. All mistakes in this work of fact, omission, interpretation, and speculation are, nevertheless, entirely my own.

*****

All Strategic Studies Institute (SSI) publications may be downloaded free of charge from the SSI website. Hard copies of this report may also be obtained free of charge while supplies last by placing an order on the SSI website. SSI publications may be quoted or reprinted in part or in full with permission and appropriate credit given to the U.S. Army Strategic Studies Institute, U.S. Army War College, Carlisle Barracks, PA. Contact SSI by visiting our website at the following address: *www.Strategic StudiesInstitute.army.mil*.

*****

The Strategic Studies Institute publishes a monthly e-mail newsletter to update the national security community on the research of our analysts, recent and forthcoming publications, and upcoming conferences sponsored by the Institute. Each newsletter also provides a strategic commentary by one of our research analysts. If you are interested in receiving this newsletter, please subscribe on the SSI website at *www.StrategicStudiesInstitute. army.mil/newsletter/*.

ISBN 1-58487-527-5

FOREWORD

In December 2011, the last U.S. combat troops were withdrawn from Iraq after an almost 9-year presence in that country. This day was welcomed by the U.S. public after years of sacrifice and struggle to build a new Iraq. Yet, the Iraq that U.S. troops have left at the insistence of its government remains a deeply troubled nation. Often Iraqi leaders view political issues in sharply sectarian terms, and national unity is elusive. The Iraqi political system was organized by both the United States and Iraq, although over time, U.S. influence diminished and Iraqi influence increased. In this monograph, Dr. W. Andrew Terrill examines the policies of de-Ba'athification as initiated by the U.S.-led Coalition Provision Authority (CPA) under Ambassador L. Paul Bremer and as practiced by various Iraqi political commissions and entities created under the CPA order. He also considers the ways in which the Iraqi de-Ba'athification program has evolved and remained an important but divisive institution over time. Dr. Terrill suggests that many U.S. officials in Iraq saw problems with de-Ba'athification, but they had difficulties softening or correcting the process once it had become firmly established in Iraqi hands. Other U.S. policymakers were slower in recognizing the politicized nature of de-Ba'athification and its devolution into a process in which both its Iraqi supporters and opponents viewed it as an instrument of Shi'ite revenge and political domination of Sunni Arabs.

Dr. Terrill's monograph considers both the future of Iraq and the differences and similarities between events in Iraq and the Arab Spring states. He has examined both Ba'athism as a concept and the ways in which it was practiced in Saddam Hussein's Iraq. He

notes that the initial principles of Ba'athism were sufficiently broad as to allow their acquisition by a tyrant
seeking ideological justification for a merciless regime. His comprehensive analysis of Iraqi Ba'athism
ensures that he does not overgeneralize when draw-
ing potential parallels to events in the Arab Spring
countries. Dr. Terrill considers the nature of Iraqi
de-Ba'athification in considerable depth and carefully
evaluates the rationales and results of actions taken
by both Americans and Iraqis involved in the process.

While there are many differences between the formation of Iraq's post-Saddam Hussein government
and the current efforts of some Arab Spring governing bodies to restructure their political institutions,
it is possible to identify parallels between Iraq and
Arab Spring countries. Some insights for emerging
governments may, correspondingly, be guided by a
comprehensive understanding of these parallels. The
Arab Spring revolutions that have overthrown the
governments of Tunisia, Egypt, Libya, and Yemen at
the time of this writing are a regional process of stun-
ning importance. While these revolutions began with
a tremendous degree of hope, great difficulties loom
in the future. New governments will have to appor-
tion power, build or reform key institutions, establish
political legitimacy for those institutions, and accom-
modate the enhanced expectations of their publics in a
post-revolutionary environment. A great deal can go
wrong in these circumstances, and it is important to
consider ways in which these new governing structures can be supported, so long as they remain inclu-
sive and democratic. Any lessons that can be gleaned
from earlier conflicts will be of considerable value to
the nations facing these problems as well as to their regional and extra-regional allies seeking to help them.

The Strategic Studies Institute is pleased to offer this monograph as a contribution to the national security debate on this important subject as our nation continues to grapple with a variety of problems associated with the future of the Middle East and the ongoing challenge of advancing U.S. interests in a time of Middle East turbulence. This analysis should be especially useful to U.S. strategic leaders and intelligence professionals as they seek to address the complicated interplay of factors related to regional security issues, the future of Iraq, and the support of local allies and emerging governments. This work may also benefit those seeking a greater understanding of long-range issues of Middle Eastern and global security. It is hoped that this work will be of benefit to officers of all services as well as other U.S. government officials involved in military and security assistance planning.

DOUGLAS C. LOVELACE, JR.
Director
Strategic Studies Institute

ABOUT THE AUTHOR

W. ANDREW TERRILL joined the Strategic Studies Institute (SSI) in October 2001, and is SSI's Middle East specialist. Prior to his appointment, he served as a Middle East nonproliferation analyst for the International Assessments Division of the Lawrence Livermore National Laboratory (LLNL). In 1998-99, Dr. Terrill also served as a Visiting Professor at the U.S. Air War College on assignment from LLNL. He is a former faculty member at Old Dominion University in Norfolk, Virginia, and has taught adjunct at a variety of other colleges and universities. He is a retired U.S. Army Reserve Lieutenant Colonel and Foreign Area Officer (Middle East). Dr. Terrill has published in numerous academic journals on topics including nuclear proliferation; the Iran-Iraq War; Operation DESERT STORM; Middle Eastern chemical weapons and ballistic missile proliferation, terrorism, and commando operations. He is also the author of *Global Security Watch-Jordan* (Praeger, 2010). Since 1994, at U.S. State Department invitation, Dr. Terrill has participated in the Middle Eastern Track 2 talks, which are part of the Middle East Peace Process. He has also served as a member of the military and security working group of the Baker/Hamilton Iraq Study Group. Dr. Terrill holds a B.A. from California State Polytechnic University and an M.A. from the University of California, Riverside, both in political science, and a Ph.D. in international relations from Claremont Graduate University, Claremont, California.

SUMMARY

The presence of U.S. combat troops in Iraq has now come to an end, and the lessons of that conflict for the United States and other nations will be debated for some time to come. It is now widely understood that the post-invasion policy of de-Ba'athification, as practiced, had numerous unintended consequences that made building Iraqi civil society especially difficult following the U.S.-led invasion. The U.S. approach to this policy is often assessed as having underestimated both the dangers of increased sectarianism in Iraq and the need for strong efforts to manage ethnic-sectarian divisions. The Iraqi government's approach to de-Ba'athification was, nevertheless, much more problematic due to its openly biased and sectarian nature. However well-intentioned, de-Ba'athification originally was as a concept, in practice it had a number of serious problems. These problems intensified and became more alarming as the de-Ba'athification process became increasingly dominated by the Iraqis and American oversight over that program gradually evaporated. At that time, it came to be viewed as an instrument of revenge and collective punishment by both the Iraqis that administered de-Ba'athification and those that were targeted by these policies.

A comprehensive review of Iraqi de-Ba'athification is necessary before making any assertions about the lessons of these policies for either Iraq or the larger Arab World. Understanding de-Ba'athification begins with a consideration of U.S. policies and goals for Iraq. After the removal of the Saddam Hussein regime, the U.S. leadership had a choice of implementing limited de-Ba'athification or seeking a much more sweeping program. They initially chose the latter course because it was deemed especially important to eliminate the last vestiges of Saddam Hussein's regime to prevent a similar type of government from reestablishing itself. In making this choice, advocates of deep de-Ba'athification pointed to the history of Ba'athist conspirators rising to power through infiltrating government institutions and seizing power in undemocratic ways. This comprehensive approach nevertheless made it extremely difficult for Iraq's Sunni Arab leaders to accept the post-war political system. Many U.S. leaders became concerned about this problem over time, but they had increasing difficulties moderating Iraqi administration of de-Ba'athification efforts.

Despite the time that has elapsed since the initial decisions on de-Ba'athification, these issues remain vital for the future of Iraq. The Sunni Arab insurgency that developed after the U.S.-led invasion reinforced the popularity of de-Ba'athification among many of Iraq's Shi'ite Arabs, thereby keeping the policy alive. Many Shi'ites also agreed with U.S. concerns about the potential emergence of a new Sunni-dominated regime that would once again seize and retain power. A quasi-legal de-Ba'athification Commission (now known as the Justice and Accountability Commission) continues to exist in Iraq and recently played a dramatic role in disqualifying some leading Sunni candidates in the 2010 parliamentary elections. This commission could not have remained relevant without the support of a variety of important Iraqi politicians, including the current prime minister. Likewise, Iraqi Prime Minister Maliki arrested large numbers of so-called "Ba'athists" in 2011, shortly before the final withdrawal of U.S. troops. Under these circumstances, the legacy of de-Ba'athification and the future of this concept within the Iraqi political system may yet have serious consequences for Iraq's ability to build a unified and successful state.

Many Americans and Iraqis of diverse political orientations have argued that de-Ba'athification and the nature of sectarianism in Iraq involved a large number of lessons that other countries may wish to consider in the context of future political transitions. This argument has found considerable resonance among some citizens in the "Arab Spring" states where popular uprisings have ousted some long-serving dictators. Many of the new revolutionaries consider Iraq's problems as a cautionary tale that must be understood as they move forward in establishing new political systems. In particular, it is now understood that loyalty commissions led by politicians and set up to identify internal enemies can take on a life of their own and become part of a nation's power structure. Once this occurs, such organizations are exceedingly difficult to disestablish. Likewise, the basic unfairness of collective punishment has again been underscored as an engine of anger, resentment, and backlash. Conversely, the importance of honest and objective judicial institutions has also been underscored, as has the importance of maintaining a distinction between revenge and justice. Moreover, officers and senior non-commissioned officers (NCOs) of the U.S. Army must realize that they may often have unique opportunities and unique credibility to offer advice on the lessons of Iraq to their counterparts in some of the Arab Spring nations. The U.S. Army has a long history of cooperating with some of the Arab Spring militaries and has a particularly strong relationship with the Egyptian military. These bonds of trust, cooperation, and teamwork can be used to convey a variety of messages beyond exclusively military issues.

All of the Arab Spring states may usefully consider the potential insights offered by events in Iraq, but the two Arab countries where the lessons of de-Ba'athification may be most relevant are Libya and Syria. Libya is currently organizing a post-Qadhafi government, while Syria is undergoing a process of revolution that seems increasingly difficult for the authorities to extinguish. In Libya, post-Qadhafi leaders are openly concerned about avoiding what they identify as the mistakes of Iraq. It remains to be seen if they are able to do so, or if they fall into new systems of internal warfare and perhaps new dictatorship. Syria maintains both a society and a style of rule that has notable similarities to the Saddam Hussein government. Its future is deeply problematic, as revolutionaries struggle against an entrenched, well-armed, and increasingly desperate dictatorial regime that is also deeply sectarian in nature.

LESSONS OF THE IRAQI DE-BA'ATHIFICATION PROGRAM FOR IRAQ'S FUTURE AND THE ARAB REVOLUTIONS

There was a tendency among promoters of the [2003-2011 Iraq] war to believe that democracy was a default condition to which societies would revert once liberated from dictators.

Francis Fukuyama[1]

I pleaded with Bremer not to dissolve the [Iraqi] army, and warned him that it would blow up in our faces. I told him that I understood the rationale behind the process of de-Baathification, but that it needed to apply only to those at the top with blood on their hands....I said I hoped he understood that if he was going to de-Baathify across the board, he would be setting himself up for major resistance and would create a power vacuum that someone would have to fill.

King Abdullah II of Jordan[2]

You cannot build a country if you don't have reconciliation and forgiveness.

Aref Ali Nayed
Libyan National
Transitional Council[3]

INTRODUCTION

The presence of U.S. combat troops in Iraq has now come to an end, and the lessons of that conflict, including those involving de-Ba'athification, will be debated for some time to come. De-Ba'athification for Iraq was initiated by U.S. policymakers in 2003 as the process of eliminating the ideology of the Iraqi Ba'ath Party from public life and removing its more influential adherents from the Iraqi political and administrative system. This policy constituted a central part of the effort to eliminate all significant aspects of the Saddamist state and remake Iraq into a democratic nation. It has also emerged as one of the most controversial aspects of U.S. post-war activities in Iraq. While supporters claim that the approach was unavoidable if Iraq was to be reformed, critics maintain that the approach, as practiced, amplified sectarian divisions in Iraq and also served as an important enabler of enhanced sectarianism and the post-invasion Iraqi insurgency.

U.S. Government decisionmaking about the nature and depth of the de-Ba'athification effort centered on the conflict between pragmatists who were attempting to prevent U.S. and Iraqi post-war authorities from losing their capacity to manage the emerging crisis in Iraq and various hardliners — often called neoconservatives — calling for a fundamental restructuring of Iraqi society. The dominant fear of the first group was that Iraq would degenerate into chaos without some effort to rehabilitate and retain those Ba'athist bureaucrats and officials not directly implicated in the Saddam Hussein regime's crimes. For the second group, the primary concern appeared to be ensuring that a favorable outcome for regime change was permanent. Their greatest fear was often that a system of "Saddamism without Saddam" would dominate the post-war environment unless large-scale societal restructuring took place within Iraq.[4] In both groups, there was a wide range of opinion, and some individuals (perhaps most prominently National Security Council [NSC] Advisor and later Secretary of State Condoleezza Rice) were open to the arguments of both sides and sought to synthesize them into coherent policy.

While de-Ba'athification still retains some defenders in the United States, most Middle Eastern politicians and observers consider it to have been deeply misguided, and many Arabs view it as a warning of the ways in which a transition from dictatorial rule can go wrong and lurch dangerously close to civil war. A strong exception to this belief can sometimes be found among Iraqi and other Arab Shi'ites, who basically approve of a policy that punishes Iraq's Sunni Arab community from which Saddam drew most of his supporters and that suffered less than other Iraqi communities under the dictatorship. The future of Iraq as a cohesive and modernizing country remains uncertain, and it is unclear if that society can overcome simmering sectarian differences, which current approaches to de-Ba'athification continue to inflame. The ways in which Iraq deals with the legacy of de-Ba'athification, as well as ongoing policies for national reconciliation, will have a great deal to do with deciding the Iraq future. While Iraqis often dream of building a society as prosperous as the Arab Gulf states, the danger remains of an Iraqi society that looks more like Lebanon during its 14-year sectarian civil war.

The onset of the Arab Spring has revived a number of questions about the problems with de-Ba'athification. At the time of this writing, Tunisia, Egypt, and Libya have experienced Arab Spring popular uprisings in which long-standing dictators have been ousted. Syria is also experiencing a serious mass uprising led by brave and extremely committed revolutionaries struggling against an entrenched and ruthlessly tenacious dictatorship. None of these states has ever experienced a government as authoritarian as Saddam Hussein's Iraq, although the Syrian dictatorship clearly comes the closest to the Saddamist model. All of these states face considerable difficulties in establishing legitimate and moderate post-revolutionary governments, and some face the danger of prolonged civil conflict. Lessons that can be gleaned from the Iraqi experience may therefore be especially important for their future.

THE BA'ATH PARTY AS AN INSTRUMENT OF SADDAM HUSSEIN'S DOMINATION OF IRAQ

In order to understand problems surrounding the effort to remove Ba'athism from Iraq, it is necessary to give some consideration to the central tenets of Ba'athism as a political ideology and then to examine the ways in which this ideology was applied and practiced within Iraq under Saddam Hussein. In undertaking this analysis, it is worthwhile to consider that a number of dictatorial regimes have used official ideologies to justify the power of a particular elite rather than to guide their actions. Some individuals within the ruling elite of such systems may view themselves as seeking to adjust their approaches to emerging problems by emphasizing those aspects of the ideology that seem most useful for addressing a given problem, while de-emphasizing those that are less useful. Such people remain ideologues despite their willingness to show a limited degree of flexibility. Others do not take the national ideology particularly seriously but value its supporting party infrastructure to justify and generate support for the decisions of the political leadership, regardless of how ideologically inconsistent those decisions may be. These people are political opportunists in ideological garb.

The Ba'ath movement was founded in the 1940s by two Syrian teachers, Michel Aflaq and Salah al-Din Bitar, and stressed Arab unity, socialism, and efforts to modernize the Arab World. The party, which emerged in its modern form in 1947, sought to unite all Arab states and to provide them with a set of modernizing principles to help them overcome problems with poverty and backwardness. The word Ba'ath means renaissance or rebirth in Arabic. The movement also sought to address the problems of the entire Arab World and was not to be confined to any individual country. Ba'athists throughout the Arab World were often viewed as committed Arab nationalists who were particularly devoted to the concept of a strong, unified Arab nation. Their slogan is, "One Arab nation with an eternal mission."

Aflaq and Bitar met at the Sorbonne in Paris, France, in 1929 where both of them became especially interested in Western literature and philosophy with an emphasis on Marxism and socialism. This form of study was a fairly conventional approach for Arab students in France, since only the French communists and socialists showed much sympathy for Syrian independence within the political spectrum of Paris in the 1930s. Moreover, Marxism's emphasis on modernization and scientific socialism appealed to the two men as they struggled for a solution to widespread Arab impoverishment and underdevelopment. The Ba'ath Party. Thus began as a secular organization seeking to modernize the Arab World in ways that were rooted in leftist, European political and social thought. Islam was not seen as a major part of this modernizing outlook. In this regard, Aflaq was not even a Muslim, having been raised as an Orthodox Christian.[5] Batar was a Sunni Muslim and, like Aflaq, had no interest in religion as a basis for the state. Within the context of Ba'athist ideology, Islam was primarily viewed as part of the Arab heritage rather than a way to organize contemporary political life. Their outlook was correspondingly deeply secular.

Like Marxist-Leninist organizations, the Ba'ath Party sought to enter power through the actions of a revolutionary elite operating in a variety of states, including Iraq. In the 1950s and 1960s, these tactics caused the Ba'ath to compete with a number of other conspiratorial movements to infiltrate the military and other centers of state power. Subversion and coups seemed the only way in which to achieve power since contested elections were almost never held in any Arab country except perhaps Lebanon. Major emerging political trends throughout the Arab World included communist and Nasserite movements as well as the Ba'ath. Thus, to achieve power within the various Arab countries Ba'athists had to operate clandestinely as one of many secretive opposition movements dealing with government counterintelligence units and their own splinter groups. Despite these difficulties, Ba'athists seized power in Syria and Iraq in 1963.[6] The Iraqi Ba'ath Party remained in power for less than a year but once again seized power in 1968 partially as a result of the maneuverings of a young revolutionary named Saddam Hussein. Additionally, the previous Iraqi government had been unable to provide significant help to the other Arab countries at war with Israel in June 1967. Iraqi Ba'athist leaders portrayed this failure as a form of treason, and made anti-Israeli invective a centerpiece of their rhetoric following their seizure of power.[7]

The Iraqi Ba'ath Party began its existence with a commitment that all party members should have a broad set of rights to elect officials and present their views in party forums. Unfortunately, this approach changed rapidly over time, and by 1964 Aflaq was complaining about the stratification of the party and the consolidation of power by a limited number of "active members" with influence that dramatically exceeded that of the rank and file. He stated that such an approach "was wholly out of keeping with the spirit of our party's rules."[8] Nevertheless, the requirement for the Ba'ath Party to carry out its activities in secret until it seized power for the second time in 1968 remained a central part of Ba'ath organizational culture throughout the organization's existence. During its underground years, the Ba'ath became increasingly hierarchical, secretive, and accustomed to violence as a political tool. These mindsets carried over to the years in power when such an approach was viewed as equally necessary to cope with real and imagined internal and foreign enemies. The Ba'ath leaders continued to see conspiracies against their government from a variety of sources including the Western powers and Israel. The failure of Iraq's first Ba'ath government to remain in power more than a year underscored the looming danger of a countercoup.

Ba'athism appeared to have some problems establishing a popular base in the first years after the 1968 coup. Some Iraqi citizens appreciated Ba'ath ideology for its emphasis on modernity and its rejection of ethnic/sectarian divisions, tribalism, and religion as the basis for a modern state. Unfortunately, in both Iraq and Syria, these principles had a more insidious function as well, helping to serve as a smokescreen for the domination of one social group over the others in each country. Secular principles in Syria were used to mask the almost complete domination of Syrian society by the Alawite minority, which is usually identified as an offshoot of Shi'ite Islam. In Iraq, the Ba'athist regime was dominated by Sunni Muslims, especially from the areas around Tikrit. The initial leader of the 1968 Ba'ath revolution in Iraq was General Ahmad Hassan al-Bakr, but he was progressively eclipsed by his young cousin, the hard-working, pragmatic, intelligent, and ruthless Saddam Hussein.

Saddam Hussein emerged as the strongman behind the scenes of the regime by the early 1970s and replaced Bakr as president in July 1979. Although Saddam permitted some loyal Shi'ites to rise to high-profile positions in government and the military, the core of his support was composed of Sunni Arabs. Shi'ite political leadership was traditionally drawn from the Iraqi Communist Party, the al-Dawa Islamiya (Islamic Call) Party, and the Shi'ite clergy. Both the Iraqi Communist Party and the Dawa Party were outlawed by the Ba'athists, and their members were ruthlessly massacred during Saddam's years in power. The Shi'ite clergy also faced massive repression under the Saddam Hussein regime, although the regime could not actually wipe them out without severe internal and regional repercussions. Instead, Saddam sought to silence the clerical leaders or force them to speak in favor of the regime. He also demanded that Sunni clerics adopt a nonpolitical role but never saw them as the same type of threat as the leading Shi'ite ayatollahs.

Saddam's relationship with Ba'athism is complex. His ability to emerge as a key Ba'athist leader is directly attributable to party co-founder, Michel Aflaq, who befriended Saddam in exile after the younger man was forced to flee Iraq following his participation in an unsuccessful assassination attempt against Iraqi President Abdul Karim Qassim. During his years outside Iraq, Saddam was able to gain Aflaq's patronage as a way to achieve high rank within the party. Saddam's ongoing relationship with Aflaq was useful to him throughout his life. Unlike the Syrian Ba'ath Party, which ousted Aflaq and Bitar from power in February 1966, Saddam remained aware of the value of maintaining Aflaq as an honored but powerless member of the Iraqi leadership. Aflaq, for his part, had hoped to be a positive and moderating influence on Saddam once the dictator achieved power, but most of his suggestions on important issues were ignored. Saddam did flatter the older man by agreeing to some of his minor concerns. Such cosmetic concessions were an acceptable trade-off for the public support of one of Ba'athism's co-founders. By consorting with the dictator, Aflaq allowed Saddam to exploit him and Ba'athism as window dressing for one of the world's most oppressive regimes. Bitar, by contrast, spent the remainder of his life in Europe. Aflaq died in 1989 in Paris, and Saddam let it be known that he used his personal funds to build a suitable tomb for the co-founder of Ba'athism.

Saddam was not a military man, and as a youth was rejected for entry into the Iraqi military academy due to poor performance on his entrance examinations.[9] Throughout his rise to power, Saddam was correspondingly wary of the danger of a military coup and used the Ba'ath Party to help him secure full control over the Army. This concern is easily understandable since coups were the traditional means of ousting an Iraqi leader once his enemies were able to organize against him. In establishing an iron grip over the military, Saddam made heavy use of Ba'athist political officers and frequently promoted cronies within the military over more qualified officers. Officers with particularly heroic reputations in the Iran-Iraq war, as well as brilliant planners, were quietly sidelined, since there was room for only one "military genius" in Saddam's Iraq. Saddam understood the value of efficient officers during times of war, but tended to place these officers in less important positions when he no longer had an immediate need for them.

The Ba'ath Party was also useful to Saddam in other ways than simply controlling the military and providing an ideological veneer for the regime. The creation of the Saddam personality cult had nothing to do with original Ba'ath ideology, but it was administered and energized by Ba'ath Party activists. As Saddam Hussein consolidated his rule over Iraq, he consistently viewed the Ba'ath Party as an instrument of dictatorial power and social mobilization. He did not take its ideology and values seriously as principles for leadership, and individuals at the highest levels were noted for their public and ostentatiously blind loyalty to the President rather than their knowledge of Ba'athist principles and political thought. While many members of the top leadership were Sunni, this was not an absolute requirement. Proven Saddam loyalists included Shi'ites, Kurds, and various sects of Christians.[10] If Saddam believed a subordinate was a proven and committed loyalist, he did not particularly care what that person's sect or ethnicity was. On the other hand, Saddam often viewed his own family and Sunni Arabs from the Tikrit area as having a head start on loyalty.[11] Saddam and his cronies also seemed to view Sunni Arabs as being more likely to remain loyal, because they were usually more hostile to the traditional enemy of Iran and were likely to fear a new Shi'ite government in which they could be viewed as accomplices in Saddam's crimes. Consequently, the Sunni Arabs were disproportionately represented in the Ba'ath's senior ranks and the regime's security units.

Once in power, the Ba'ath Party did follow through on some of its modernization rhetoric. Saddam was committed to building a modern state, although he basically sought this goal primarily to improve the efficiency of the dictatorship rather than to benefit the Iraqi people. Consequently, serious and intense Ba'ath Party literacy drives did more than teach Iraqi citizens how to read.[12] They also opened an intellectual pathway that allowed them to be more thoroughly bombarded with regime propaganda. Efforts to reduce the power of the tribes and to limit the role of religion in public life were similarly presented as modernization efforts, although their primary purpose was to further centralize power in Baghdad. Moreover, such policies could be reversed when they were no longer convenient to the regime, as occurred in the late 1980s and throughout the 1990s when Saddam's regime sought to encourage some increased religious devotion, so long as such sentiments were properly channeled into activities that the regime viewed as useful.[13] Additionally, Saddam was also willing to work through tribal elements when it suited his purposes.

On the eve of the 2003 U.S.-led invasion, Saddam's Iraq was a one of the most rigid totalitarian states in the world, with a privileged elite composed of military leaders and Ba'ath Party members, virtually all of whom were terrified of the leader.[14] The Ba'ath Party had at least two million members at that time, with some estimates reaching 2.5 million. Nevertheless, membership in the senior ranks of the Ba'ath Party did not protect individuals from Saddam's terror, which was applied to them to ensure that rival centers of power did not develop within the party.[15] Saddam was particular wary of ambitious "overachievers" who might be interested in political advancement in ways that could eventually lead to the rise of political competitors. He was also deeply wary of those officials who began to appear too pious. Saddam further had an occasional need for visible Ba'athist victims to reinforce the determination of the remaining Ba'athists to show unquestioning obedience and subservience. Senior leaders such as Tariq Aziz were sometimes publicly embarrassed by Saddam, as when he was told to lose weight and had his weekly progress reported in the newspaper.[16] More ominously, a casual joke about Saddam or his priorities could result in the loss of a senior leader's tongue.[17] Everyone within the Iraqi political leadership understood that they had no rights that Saddam could not immediately nullify if he chose to do so for whatever reason. This principle applied to the top elite as well as the oppressed masses. Thus, when Saddam was ousted in 2003, some Ba'athists as well as non-Ba'athists were open to the idea of participating in the building of a new Iraq if they had the opportunity. The most likely exceptions to this approach would be those Ba'athists who were implicated in Saddam's crimes. These people knew there would never be any kind of future for them in an Iraq without Saddam or at least a Saddamist type of system.

THE DE-BA'ATHIFICATION ORDER OF MAY 16, 2003

Under the circumstances noted above, the Iraq population was confused and uncertain about what would happen to the Ba'athists once Saddam's regime was removed from power. While General Tommy Franks had abolished the Ba'ath Party in a 2003 message to the Iraqi people, he gave little indication of how individual Ba'athists outside of Iraq's top circles would be treated. In the immediate aftermath of Saddam's ouster, both the U.S. military and the newly established Organization for Reconstruction and Humanitarian Assistance (ORHA) seemed to be showing some clear flexibility. ORHA was willing to allow former Ba'athist administrators and professionals such as doctors and professors to keep their jobs so long as they were not implicated in regime crimes and were willing to renounce their previous Ba'athist affiliations.[18] This approach was viewed as necessary to keep the economy from further declining or even collapsing. The U.S. Army also showed considerable pragmatism by sponsoring renunciation ceremonies in which thousands of people burned their Ba'ath membership cards, renounced violence, and pledged to help build the new Iraq.[19] This approach was particularly successful in the area around Mosul, where then Major General David Petraeus presided over such ceremonies. Mosul, at this time, remained quiet, despite its tradition of supplying large numbers of Sunni Arab officers to the Iraqi military. Later, after more comprehensive de-Ba'athification policies were instituted over the objection of the U.S. military leadership there, everything changed, Mosul became much more difficult to manage, and a strong al-Qaeda presence was established in the region.

As noted above, the more tolerant approach of ORHA was not to last. An order to de-Ba'athify Iraqi society was the first major official act of Ambassador L. Paul Bremer upon his arrival in that country to assume control of the newly created Coalition Provisional Authority (CPA), which replaced ORHA. Bremer issued this order on May 16, 2003, after being provided with the directive in draft form by Undersecretary of Defense for Policy Douglas Feith. According to Bremer, Feith told him that such an order was absolutely essential to Iraq's rehabilitation.[20] The order disestablished the Ba'ath Party and removed members of the four highest ranks of the party from government positions. It also banned them from future employment in the public sector. Additionally, the order required that anyone holding positions in the top three management layers in government institutions be interviewed to determine their level of involvement with the Ba'ath Party as well as their possible involvement in criminal activities. Those determined to be senior members of the party were to be removed from their positions and banned from any future public employment. The order also called for the creation of a rewards program to pay individuals providing information leading to the capture of senior Ba'ath Party members.

The supporters of the de-Ba'athification program frequently maintained that this approach was inspired by the de-Nazification efforts that followed World War II in Germany. Iraqi exiles were fond of the term, which they may have viewed as loaded in a way that made it a useful public relations tool to advocate war and to help clear a way for prominent roles for themselves in the new Iraq. Additionally, some U.S. senior officials had, by this time, begun viewing Iraq through the lens of Nazi Germany with Saddam as Hitler and the Ba'ath Party as the Nazis.[21] Such analogies correctly point out the moral repugnancy of the Saddam Hussein regime, but they also allow one to glance over the particulars of Iraqi society and argue about Iraq's future on the basis of analogies rather than conditions within Iraq itself. In just one important difference, it may be significant that the Nazis rose to power as a large and powerful mass movement, whereas the

Ba'athists rose to power in Iraq through the actions of a group of conspirators. Individuals joining the Ba'ath movement after it seized power may have done so with motives other than loyalty to Saddam Hussein.

The de-Ba'athification order and the subsequent CPA Order #2 (issued shortly afterward on May 23 to disband Iraq's military and intelligence forces) reflect the priorities of both Under Secretary Feith and Deputy Secretary of Defense Paul Wolfowitz. These priorities centered on the destruction of all forces previously involved in supporting the old regime and particularly those forces that they believed had a chance of reconstituting that regime. The Ba'ath had a long history of underground activity as well as a past pattern of infiltrating key institutions and then attempting to seize power by illegal means. The revival of Ba'athism through conspiracy and intrigue therefore seemed a realistic danger. Unfortunately, such a revival was not the only serious danger facing Iraq at this time, and it was not clearly so dangerous as to trump all other security concerns. It is also not clear if the U.S. leadership fully understood the numbers of enemies that they were making by undertaking such policies or the backlash such actions could produce. The possibility that such a backlash could lead to a serious Sunni military challenge to the new Iraq was apparently dismissed on the grounds that such "dead-enders" were a marginalized force and would not be able to establish a popular rather than a conspiratorial movement within Iraqi society. Ahmad Hashim, in his insightful study of the Iraqi insurgency, quotes an anonymous U.S. policymaker as stating, "We underestimated their [the Iraqis] capacity to put up resistance. We underestimated the role of nationalism. And we overestimated the appeal of liberation [as trumping all other considerations for Iraqi political behavior]."[22] Another even more biting critic stated that the civilians within the George Bush administration had made the fundamental mistake of confusing strategy with ideology.[23]

Some authors also claim that the CPA's policies were deliberately anti-Sunni and pro-Shi'ite because of a belief within the Bush administration that Sunnis were more dangerous to U.S. interests, while Shi'ites were more likely to be grateful to the United States for ousting Saddam, since they had suffered more under his regime.[24] This charge about administration policy-making is more popular in the Arab World than in the United States and is difficult to confirm. Some Bush policymakers did speak forcefully against Sunni control in Iraq, but they justified their concerns around the theme of democracy rather than the inherent untrustworthiness of the Sunni Arabs.[25] In some regional media, as well as in Iraq, the de-Ba'athification policy was sometimes referred to as "de-Arabization."[26] The central tenets of the Ba'ath Party are Arab nationalism, anti-imperialism, and Arab socialism. Such ideals are not usually viewed as offensive by themselves, and many Arabs consider them to be noble and praiseworthy. Treating Ba'athism, instead of Saddam's version of Ba'athism, as corrupt was therefore a problem for many Arabs and the pan-Arab media including the satellite television stations where Iraqis often sought to get the news.

In an effort that further complicated the situation, some leading Iraqi Shi'ites attempted to play upon U.S. fears by suggesting that Sunnis were "Arab nationalists." This is a label that is seldom viewed as a slur in the Arab World, but in this instance was apparently used to suggest an anti-American and anti-

Israeli worldview. Throughout the years following the invasion, some Shi'ite leaders consistently sought to convey the view that Sunnis were irredeemably wedded to radicalism, and needed to be marginalized to protect both Iraqi and Shi'ite interests. In one particularly revealing incident, Shi'ite leader Abdulaziz Hakim made it clear that he supported democracy so long as his organization and sect benefited from that democracy. In conversations reported by journalist Bob Woodward and others, Hakim told members of the Baker/Hamilton Iraq Study Group that the government of Iraq represented 80 percent of the population of that country (Shi'ites and Kurds) so democracy was served, and nothing had to be done about the remaining Sunnis.[27]

When Bremer informed the senior staff of the CPA (and especially the ORHA holdovers) of the new de-Ba'athification approach, he met immediate resistance over the scope of the order that he had brought from Washington. Retired Lieutenant General Jay Garner, the outgoing Director of ORHA, was reported to have been disturbed by the order, which he characterized as "too deep."[28] Charlie Sidell, the Baghdad Central Intelligence Agency (CIA) Chief of Station who worked with Garner during this period, stated, "Well if you do this, you're going to drive 30,000 to 50,000 Ba'athists underground by nightfall, and the number is closer to 50,000 than it is to 30,000."[29] Garner and Sidell went to Bremer to attempt to dissuade him from issuing the order until it had been moderated to reflect the realities that they were facing. They recommended eliminating the top two levels of Ba'athist leadership, which was about 6,000 people.[30] According to Garner, Bremer stated, "Look, I have my orders. This is what I am doing."[31] Since Bremer held the rank of Presidential Envoy in direct communication with the President, it is not immediately clear who issued such orders. Undersecretary Feith could not have done so on his own authority. President Bush had previously given Defense Secretary Donald Rumsfeld managerial control of the occupation, so it is possible that Feith spoke for Rumsfeld who spoke for Bush and Vice President Dick Cheney.[32] A complicating factor in this situation is that throughout his time in office, Bremer was willing to ignore the advice of the Defense and State Departments on other issues later in his tenure. If he did not do so in this instance, he probably believed in the policy that was being put forward or considered it to have come directly from the President. It is also likely that he did not fully understand the importance of the advice he was receiving from Garner and the CIA, since he later stated that he did not recall the conversation.[33] Garner left Iraq shortly afterward, sharing his concerns over de-Ba'athification with U.S. Central Command (CENTCOM) Deputy Commander then Lieutenant General John Abizaid, who also feared that the deep de-Ba'athification effort would feed the developing resistance.[34] General Abizaid would become CENTCOM commander after General Franks' retirement.

In a related event, President Bush later appeared to blame Bremer for disbanding the Iraqi Army (although not for deep de-Ba'athification), suggesting that presidential guidance on one of the most important issues of the occupation was not reflected in CPA decisionmaking. Rather, Bush told journalist Robert Draper, "The policy had been to keep the [Iraqi] army intact. Didn't happen."[35] Bremer responded angrily to the President's statement, saying that he had been ordered to disband the Army by Rumsfeld, and the

White House had approved the move. He also made the unusual claim that disbanding the Iraqi Army had been the correct choice, but he was not the one responsible for this decision.[36] Clearly, these are very different versions of the truth, and no one wants to take responsibility for disbanding Iraqi security forces in spite of Bremer's professed belief that it had been the correct approach. Despite this inconsistency, Bremer's arguments have a certain level of resonance, since it is difficult to believe that he would have implemented such dramatic policy changes without at least a general understanding of President Bush's priorities on de-Ba'athification and the future of the Iraqi military.

At this point, Bremer was imposing Washington's priorities and appeared primarily concerned about preventing the possible reconstitution of the Ba'ath regime. These fears may have been enhanced by Saddam's status as a fugitive at that time. Moreover, Bremer also entered Iraq with the determination to establish himself quickly as a decisive leader willing to make decisions that were unpopular with his staff, the military, and others in the U.S. Government. In his book, Bremer relates an incident in which his son gave him a pair of desert combat boots as a going away gift with the note that they were to help him "kick some butt."[37] He was apparently in total agreement with that sentiment.[38] Bremer clearly felt that asserting his will over subordinates was exceptionally important if he was to maintain effective control of the CPA and Iraqi policy.[39] He made this effort in the face of considerable local unhappiness about CPA policy, and de-Ba'athification was especially unpopular in the U.S. military because U.S. officers lost their hardest working and most competent counterparts.[40] In response to the order, some commanders, and most notably General Petraeus, sought wide authority to grant waivers from the de-Ba'athificaiton requirements for local individuals to limit the disruptions caused by this policy.[41]

Bremer claims in his book that he expected the de-Ba'athification order to be applied to only about 20,000 people, or what he identified as 1 percent of all party members. The program would therefore include the ranks officially designated as "Senior Party Members." Bremer also claims to have been sensitive to the needs of lower-ranking Ba'ath Party members to join the organization to make a living. He later maintained that his order was applied in ways that he never intended, and that many more people were purged than he had envisioned under the original program. This included people of much lower rank than the levels of Ba'ath membership outlined in the order as well as individuals whose links to the Ba'ath Party leadership were tenuous at best. He was also apparently unresponsive to Ambassador Barbara Bodine's argument made earlier to General Garner that some senior members of the party were not criminals, while various junior members had engaged in serious crimes, making a blanket approach based on rank alone unfair and ineffective.[42]

Another problem for the CPA was that the justice of the de-Ba'athification order was not clear to many Iraqis. Joining the Ba'ath Party in Saddam's Iraq was a rational decision for anyone seeking to feed their family and live in conditions other than squalor and poverty. The best and most numerous jobs in Iraq are found in the government and in state-controlled enterprises such as the oil industry. In Iraq, as in most Middle Eastern countries, there is not a strong private sector with a wide variety of good jobs. Socialism and state control of the economy were official parts of the Ba'ath ideology, further weakening the nongovernmental sector, while years of United Nations (UN) sanctions (1990-2003) undermined foreign investment in the Iraqi economy and also retarded private sector development. Yet, it is also within the government that one was most vulnerable to pressure to show enthusiasm for Saddam's rule. In this environment, the greatest and most direct system of rewards and punishment had been put into place for rewarding loyalty to the government and the party. In Iraq, a non-Ba'athist primary school teacher would usually be paid the equivalent of U.S. $4 per month, while a Ba'athist in the same position, doing the same work, would be paid around $200 per month.[43]

Unfortunately, Bremer's estimate of 20,000 people being purged as a result of his order did not hold up. While exact numbers are impossible to obtain, most estimates place the number as at least 30,000 and possibly up to 50,000 individuals.[44] A few estimates place it even higher and note that the party members' families, as well as ousted Ba'athists, were harmed by the mass firings.[45] Blanket de-Ba'athification punished Iraq's managerial class merely for being part of that class, and not because of individual misconduct, abuse of power, or other crimes. Moreover, other choices were available to address the problem, although they clearly would have been more cumbersome. According to one observer, the best alternative would have been to place the Ba'athists on trial and then punish those found guilty of human rights violations, corruption, incompetence, and other crimes. A truth and reconciliation commission could then have been established along South African lines. Such an option would have avoided the approach of treating all Ba'athists in responsible positions as criminals.[46] Additionally, there was also the possibility supported by Garner and others to dismiss only the top two levels of the Ba'ath Party leadership and thereby try to avoid plunging Iraq into an administrative vacuum by eliminating managers and technocrats, many of whom were only "nominal Ba'athists."[47]

As will be examined later, Bremer maintains that his de-Ba'athification order was issued with a full understanding of the complexities of Iraqi society, but it was overzealously applied. Yet, if Bremer's authority and the approach of his order were abused, he still cannot be fully absolved for the difficulties that followed. In addition to problems with the decision itself, it is unclear that the CPA leadership paid enough attention to how his order was being implemented throughout the process rather than simply issuing a fiat and expecting it to be carried forward without difficulty, first under the authority of the CPA and then by the Iraqi government. Lieutenant General Ricardo Sanchez, a former commander in Iraq, excoriated the CPA on these grounds noting, "[T]he CPA treated [de-Ba'athification] like they were issuing an academic, theoretical paper. They simply released the order and declared success. But there was no vision, no concept, and in my opinion, no desire to ensure that the policy was properly implemented. On the other hand, it did look good on paper."[48]

While Bremer was to become more pragmatic over time, his first few days in Iraq resulted in what have arguably emerged as some of the worst mistakes associated with the war, and these mistakes were impossible to reverse by the time he started to understand their negative implications.[49] It is nevertheless also useful to understand the context of Bremer's actions by looking at the reaction to these policies in Washington. In his memoir, Douglas Feith minimizes the chaos created by de-Ba'athification, and takes issue with Bremer's later second thoughts about the policy.[50] Unlike Bremer, he was unprepared to admit that the de-Ba'athification policy may have been producing bad results. Rather than adjust his focus to the real and emerging problems as Bremer eventually did, Feith, at least publicly, continued to support policies that were proving disastrous.

ADMINISTRATION OF THE DE-BA'ATHIFICATION PROGRAM

Nine days after the issuance of CPA Order Number 1, Bremer established a de-Ba'athification Council, which he was to supervise and which would report "directly and solely" to him.[51] Later, on November 3, 2003, the responsibility for implementing de-Ba'athification was passed from the CPA to the U.S.-created Iraqi Governing Council (IGC).[52] The IGC made de-Ba'athification the responsibility of Governing Council member Ahmad Chalabi, who was placed in charge of the newly-created "Supreme National Commission for De-Ba'athification." Chalabi was supported in his efforts at deep de-Ba'athification by the Shi'ite religious parties such as Dawa and the Supreme Council for the Islamic Revolution in Iraq (SCIRI, later the Islamic Supreme Council of Iraq) and by various Kurdish groups. Former post-Saddam Defense Minister Ali Allawi (not to be confused with Ayad Allawi) describes Iraqi Kurds as favoring broad de-Ba'athification, but with so many exceptions that their actual priorities were difficult to sort out.[53] Most Sunni Iraqi Arabs did not favor deep de-Ba'athification, although many of them had also suffered under Saddam Hussein. Additionally, it did not escape Sunni Arab attention that the primary Iraqi champions of deep de-Ba'athification were formerly exiled Shi'ite politicians such as Ahmad Chalabi of the Iraqi National Congress and Abdul Azziz Hakim of SCIRI. Many Sunni Iraqi Arabs considered "de-Ba'athification" to be synonymous with "de-Sunnization," a strong and deliberate effort to marginalize the role of the Sunni Arab community in Iraq's political future.[54]

The de-Ba'athification process impacted every important aspect of Iraqi economic life, due to the centrality of state-run enterprises to the Iraqi economy. These included the educational system, utilities, food distribution centers, and the oil industry. The possibility that Ba'athists would be educating young people was of special concern to those in favor of deep de-Ba'athification. Consequently, the de-Ba'athification order was used to justify the immediate firing of 1,700 university professors and staff throughout Iraq, although no one maintained that they were all complicit in Saddam's crimes or even that they were committed Ba'ath ideologues.[55] Rather, they were often simply attempting to get by within the Saddamist system that permeated the state. The post-Saddam former prime minister Ayad Allawi has referred to this approach as Iraqi citizens using Ba'athist membership as a "vehicle to live."[56] Later, Bremer expressed unhappiness that "tens of thousands" of school teachers (K-12) had been dismissed from their jobs, even though they were only low-ranking members of the Ba'ath Party who had been forced to join as a condition of their employment.[57] He strongly disapproved of such actions, but by this time much of the de-Ba'athification process had moved out of his direct control and was being managed by either Chalabi or by local committees that had set themselves up using Bremer's order as the rationale for their activities. Chalabi, who had strong allies in the U.S. civilian leadership of the Pentagon, may have been particularly difficult for Bremer to moderate. Much later, in retrospect, Bremer indicated that de-Ba'athification should have been conducted by a judicial body rather than a commission led by Iraqi politicians.[58]

The collapse of large segments of the Iraqi educational system harmed not only teachers but students and Iraqi families by rendering schools and universities increasingly dysfunctional. It also created pools of high school and college age males who could sometimes be approached about the possibility of participating in the insurgency. Other state-controlled bureaucracies were decapitated as well, but these leadership gaps did not always last for long. In the south and the Shi'ite sections of Baghdad, Shi'ite clergy and their supporters quickly established their leadership over a variety of local government institutions.[59] Many of these people were affiliated with Muqtada Sadr's Sadr II movement (so named to indicate continuity with his murdered father's charitable activities). Holdover officials within the establishments seized by the Sadrists or other groups were quickly made to feel unwelcome or even in danger unless they pledged loyalty to the new leadership. These new political leaders often had no concept of the technical or administrative issues associated with the enterprises that they seized. Nevertheless, the rise of Shi'ite clerics to fill the political vacuum in their own community is not surprising. The Shi'ite political establishment was one of the only organized forces outside of the Ba'ath Party in Iraq at the time of the invasion. Moreover, it had a strong and loyal following, a system of self-financing, and a record of long-standing persecution by the regime. Later, the Sadrists lost some of their initial power following Muqtada Sadr's political and military confrontations with the Iraq government led by rival Shi'ite politician Nuri al-Maliki.

Many Ba'athists who held ranks below the highest four levels of the Ba'ath Party were also purged under the 2003 de-Ba'athification order, because it was often difficult to discern an individual's rank within the Ba'ath Party. Often such standing was not clear to those around the person, and a large number of records were destroyed in the immediate aftermath of the invasion and the looting of Iraqi government offices that occurred following the fall of the Saddam regime. Individuals who held important administrative positions were therefore often simply assumed to be high-ranking Ba'athists and removed from office. Ironically, some individuals who were not important in the Ba'ath Party were strong pro-Saddam sympathizers, while some important Ba'athists sought to rise within the Iraqi government and bureaucracy through whatever means available. Allowing junior officials to assume the jobs of their former superiors did not necessarily lead to a bureaucracy that was inherently more anti-Saddam or pro-democracy.

The decision to place Chalabi in charge of the de-Ba'athification process was also unfortunate. At least some U.S. leaders were aware of exactly what they were getting with a Chalabi-led de-Ba'athification Commission, and they should have understood that he was not likely to show restraint on this issue.[60] Chalabi had been an advocate for wide-ranging de-Ba'athification well before the war against Saddam had begun in 2003. He had previously published his concerns that the United States would invade Iraq but would not attempt to eliminate all aspects of the Ba'ath Party with the comprehensiveness that he favored. In a February 19, 2002, *Wall Street Journal* editorial, Chalabi attacked what he called the plans for the future occupation of Iraq, which he apparently believed he understood on the basis of testimony before Congress by U.S. military and Bush administration officials. According to Chalabi, "[T]he proposed U.S. occupation and military administration of Iraq is unworkable. Unworkable because it is predicated on keeping Saddam's existing structures of government in place—albeit under American officers."[61] He went on to claim that, "Iraq needs a comprehensive program of de-Ba'athification even more extensive than the de-Nazification effort in Germany after World War II."

Chalabi has often been identified as the least popular member of the Governing Council among the Iraqi population at the time of his appointment by the IGC to head the de-Ba'athification Commission. His status as an exile caused at least some to view him as an outsider who had no experiences of the challenge of living under Saddam.[62] The strong and public ties Chalabi held to both Israelis and pro-Israeli figures in the U.S. Government were well-known and not universally appreciated throughout Iraq.[63] Later, the December 2005 elections underscored his unpopularity when his political party failed to win a single seat in the 475-person Parliament, despite a massive political campaign under the slogan, "We Liberated Iraq."[64] The decision to move forward with Chalabi at the head of the Commission rather than seeking a more reconciliation-oriented figure indicated a continuing determination to impose a harsh peace on the Sunnis and anyone associated with the old regime.

This approach was consistent with the priorities of the senior Pentagon civilians who remained concerned that a regime similar to the one led by Saddam could reemerge. This danger was also worrisome to many of Iraq's Shi'ite and Kurdish leaders who were aware that the Ba'ath had previously come to power twice through coups.

As noted, the Shi'ite religious parties and other community leaders were among the groups most interested in comprehensive de-Ba'athification priorities. U.S. policymakers seeking to justify a more sweeping de-Ba'athification policy were quick to point out that failure to do this would potentially harm U.S. relations with these parties.[65] Nor is it difficult to understand the intense hatred Shi'ites and Kurds held for Saddam and the Ba'ath. Shi'ite religious parties, as well as the Shi'ite-dominated Iraqi Communist Party, had suffered intensively under Saddam, and most prominent members of these organizations had lost a number of friends and family members to torture and execution by the regime. The rise of a Shi'ite Islamic republic in Iran through revolution was particularly frightening to Saddam, who unleashed an especially high level of brutality against Iraqi Shi'ites who seemed even the slightest bit comfortable with the Iranian concept of Islamic government. An overly political definition of Shi'ite identity during the 1980-88 Iran-Iraq war was especially dangerous. Nevertheless, revenge (or justice) was not the only motivation for the Shi'ite parties in supporting de-Ba'athification. Many of these groups also wanted as much power as possible for themselves. Destroying the political viability of the Sunni leadership in Iraq helped to move them toward that goal. Some Shi'ite leaders may have also hoped to reverse the situations of Sunnis and Shi'ites permanently. In contrast to Iraq's first 8 decades of existence, Shi'ites would hold the important positions, and Sunnis would be politically marginalized. Under these circumstances, some Sunni Arabs believed that they were being offered second-class citizenship at best.

The CPA de-Ba'athification order was sometimes taken as at least a partial green light for some Iraqis to exact revenge on former Ba'athists who had persecuted them or were their personal enemies. Indeed, a Shi'ite assassination campaign against former Ba'athists did take place, although it is doubtful that a more reconciliationist approach by the CPA would have prevented these outbreaks of violence, once the dictatorship had been removed. [66] Many of these assassinations were carried forward in a highly professional manner, rather than as frenzy or sloppy revenge attacks. It is correspondingly possible, if not likely, that Iranian intelligence units coordinated with friendly Shi'ite groups to ensure that Ba'athist enemies of Tehran were never in a position for them to cause trouble for Iran again.[67] According to the London-based newsmagazine, *The Middle East,* Iranian Supreme leader Ali Khamenei put the commander of the al-Quds Force in charge of setting up a network of covert operatives in Iraq as early as September 2002, with the mission of expanding Iranian influence in that country in the aftermath of the invasion.[68]

If Chalabi hoped to use the de-Ba'athification Commission as an avenue for his own rise to power, he was deeply disappointed by the outcome of the 2005 election. While he may have helped to create a power vacuum by purging a number of potential rivals, he did not have the ability to fill it through the electoral process. Rather, the most important players in Iraq at this stage were quickly proven to be the Shi'ite religious parties who were also enthusiastic supporters of de-Ba'athification. After the election, Chalabi moved in and out of a variety of governmental jobs, which he held for various lengths of time. Throughout his political maneuvering, he was unable to obtain real power within the top leadership of the government.

As noted above, many Iraqi Sunnis viewed the effort to remove large numbers of Sunni leaders and bureaucrats from power through the vehicle of de-Ba'athification as part of a new political system in which Shi'ites would dominate Sunnis. The politicization of sectarian differences also led Iraqi political parties to adapt an approach whereby they viewed failing to fill a political post with one of your supporters or allies as tantamount to allowing that post to be filled by enemies.[69] In addition to Sunni Muslims, some "establishment Shi'ites" had also risen to high ranks within the Ba'ath Party and were also caught up in de-Ba'athification. A key problem here is that Saddam actively reached out to secular Shi'ites to serve as "democratic ornaments," while attempting to marginalize the Shi'ite clergy, which he felt was at least potentially loyal to Iran.[70] Some secular Shi'ite leaders, including those with advanced degrees from Western universities, took the bait for a variety of reasons including the hope that they could gain some reasonable level of patronage for their own communities. Some of these people were also well-educated and talented enough to be of real use to the regime in performing administrative tasks. These links with the regime allowed such individuals to become targets for de-Ba'athification in ways that the more persecuted opposition clerics did not once the regime had been removed.[71]

The most prominent example of the problems faced by "establishment Shi'ites" was the case of Saadoun Hammadi, the former Iraqi premier who died of leukemia in Germany in March 2007.[72] Saadoun Hammadi had previously served as Iraq's Foreign Minister, Deputy Prime Minister, Prime Minister, and most recently, Saddam's last Speaker of the Assembly, thus becoming the highest ranking Shi'ite within the regime. Hammadi held a Ph.D. in economics from the University of Wisconsin and has been described as having a "thoughtful and scholarly demeanor."[73] He also is the author of a number of academic articles on Arab affairs and political philosophy.[74] Hammadi favored economic and political liberalism in the past, and was presented to the world as a reform prime minister after the 1991 Gulf War. He apparently took his reform charter a little too seriously for Saddam and was removed for overzealousness after 7 months in power.[75]

As an articulate, respected Shi'ite intellectual who held high-profile/high-prestige government positions, Hammadi helped give Saddam's government the appearance of broad-based Iraqi support across religious sects. Saddam thus presented Hammadi with the option of being co-opted and in return gaining a few crumbs of power for himself and some economic assistance for his Shi'ite supporters. This Faustian bargain was occasionally made available to Western-educated secular intellectuals, but it was almost never an option for important members of the Shi'ite clergy. Although Saddam sometimes sought to appear religious, formal clerical participation in the Ba'athist government was largely unacceptable to him. Certainly, no ayatollah would hold any of the governmental positions Hammadi held. Hammadi was arrested and placed in prison shortly after the U.S.-led invasion, while his son and members of his al-Karakshah tribe stringently protested his arrest on grounds that he did

31

not take part in any crime against the Iraqi people.[76] He was released in February 2004, in partial response to the uproar within the Shi'ite community. He then traveled to a series of Arab countries and then to Germany where he died.

Other secular Shi'ite leaders were also tarnished by their association with Saddam's government, although they collaborated for a mix of personal, communal, and national motives. They were, however, not always subject to the same level of punishment as Sunni Ba'athists. According to the International Crisis Group (ICG), Shi'ite political parties involved with the de-Ba'athification process often allowed Shi'ite Ba'ath Party members to repent and keep their jobs. In doing so, the former Ba'athists became subservient to the parties that allowed them to remain in their positions and vulnerable to pressure from these parties so long as they remained a relevant political force.[77] Any former Ba'athists showing much independence from the new political leadership at this stage usually found themselves accused of leaking information to terrorists or a variety of other crimes, regardless of whether or not they had done anything wrong. De-Ba'athification consequently may have helped the Shi'ite clergy and religious parties establish almost full control over the Shi'ite community during the first years following the invasion. While Shi'ite secularists, including those associated with the Ba'ath, were not punished to the extent of Sunni Ba'athists under de-Ba'athification, they were also not in a position to seek the leadership of the Shi'ite community. At this time, there seemed to be limited room for a reformed anti-Iranian secularist leadership that included ex-Ba'athists in Iraq.[78]

The removal of Ba'athist officials also created problems in finding suitable replacements with satisfactory political credentials. Some individuals who had been fired by Ba'athists from various bureaucracies under the Ba'athist regime became strong candidates to replace them following the change of regime. The problem here is that such individuals sometimes (perhaps often) were fired for nonpolitical reasons, including incompetence and corruption. Upon being returned to their former jobs or those of their former supervisors, they returned to old patterns of behavior, showing little responsibility, effectiveness, or commitment to even a limited work ethic. To be fair, it might be noted that these people had no monopoly on the shortcomings noted here. Most Iraqis had never had any preparation to work in an efficient, modernizing bureaucracy, and corruption permeated the society during the Saddam years as it still does.[79]

At various times, the Iraqi government announced that it was relaxing the de-Ba'athificiation policy, often as a response to U.S. pressure. Chalabi would usually announce the policy "changes" and then provide grandiose projections of how many people would be rehabilitated under new more lenient rules. In early 2007, for instance, he publicly agreed to soften the de-Ba'athification policy, announcing that his office had begun removing hiring restrictions from former Ba'athists who had not committed crimes during the Saddam years. Elaborating on this change, he stated that more than 2,300 former high-ranking Ba'ath Party members were either being reinstated in their former jobs or granted pensions.[80] On the same day, Chalabi stated that over 700 former Ba'athists had returned to their old government jobs, suggesting that the balance of the 2,300 people he cited were given pensions if his figures are correct.[81] Chalabi's commitment to reform nevertheless remained tactical, and there is no independent evidence for the figures he cited. Additionally, Chalabi opposed any new law on de-Ba'athification that would contain a sunset clause that would abolish the commission at some future point.[82]

An interesting window into the impartiality of the de-Ba'athification process occurred with the August 2008 arrest of Ali Faisal al-Lami, then the executive director of the de-Ba'athification Commission. Al-Lami was arrested as he returned home from Lebanon as a "suspected senior special group leader," according to journalistic sources.[83] Various offshoots of Muqtada al-Sadr's Mahdi Army and other pro-Iranian terrorist organizations are known as "special groups" and are among the most extreme forces within the Iraqi political system. Some of these groups are controlled by Iranian intelligence organizations such as the al-Quds Force.[84] The idea that someone comfortable with this ideology was presiding over de-Ba'athification is bone-chilling. Chalabi nevertheless demanded al-Lami's release following the arrest.[85] He stated that al-Lami played "a great essential role [in] fighting and confronting Saddam's regime despite the risks that surrounded him."[86] He further added that U.S. forces pay "no attention to Iraqi human rights." While many details of this situation were not disclosed and al-Lami's guilt remained publicly unproven, his purported admiration for Tehran further reinforced the image of the de-Ba'athification Commission as hopelessly biased against Sunni Arabs. Al-Lami remained in detention until August 2009, when he was released as part of an agreement between the Iraqi government and various Shi'ite parties.[87] After his release, al-Lami returned to political and de-Ba'athification activities, as noted later in this monograph. Al-Lami's role in de-Ba'athification ended in May 2011 when he was assassinated by unknown gunmen who were probably members of al-Qaeda.[88]

MILITARY IMPLICATIONS OF DE-BA'ATHIFICATION

The decision to dissolve the Iraqi Army and the Ba'ath Party within the first few days of establishing the CPA administered an overwhelming blow to organized Iraqi life. This radical shock therapy was deemed by some members of the Bush administration as vital to the establishment of a stable democracy in Iraq. Of all of the CPA actions in this time frame, the abolition of the Iraqi Army was the most controversial and disconcerting to many Iraqis, who often viewed the military as something more than a pillar of the Saddam Hussein regime. Supporters of the decision often claim that the Iraqi Army dissolved itself, and that the reality of the post-war situation was simply being recognized. This argument implies that the United States only had only two choices, reconstituting the 600,000-man Iraqi Army in its Saddamist form or bringing the Iraqi Army down to zero. The choice, however, was never that binary, and the CPA order was issued at a point when U.S. Army General David D. McKiernan and various CIA officials were already working on a third option, that of reconstituting certain units of the Iraqi military on a voluntary basis under vetted officers.[89] These efforts had to be discontinued following the CPA announcement.

Armed resistance to U.S. forces at some level following the invasion was probably inevitable, no matter how well the post-war reconstruction effort was handled. The question was, would this resistance comprise small groups of terrorists or would it encompass much larger forces drawn from alienated social groups that were able to organize into a strong network of resistance organizations. At this stage in the conflict, the Bush administration was loath to admit that segments of the Iraqi population were waging war against U.S. forces rather than welcoming them. At a June 2003 press conference, Secretary of Defense Rumsfeld stated, "I guess the reason I don't use the phrase 'guerrilla war' is because there isn't one."[90] In general, the administration seemed to believe that the Iraqis would be sufficiently grateful for liberation that they would be granted sweeping ability to do anything they wanted in Iraq without much of a backlash.[91] This view was emphatically reinforced by some of the most pro-war Iraqi exiles who maintained that Iraqis were so oppressed that they did not care about much else other than their deliverance from Saddam Hussein.[92]

The de-Ba'athification order, as unpopular as it was with Sunni Arab Iraqis, was not as unpopular as the disbanding of the Iraqi Army. Yet, if the United States was determined to implement a de-Ba'athification order, the rationale for dissolving the Army becomes much less clear. Senior Ba'athist officers could have been retired under the de-Ba'athification order, and low-ranking Ba'athists and non-Ba'athists could have been offered the option to remain in the military provided that they were not complicit in regime crimes. Ba'ath political officers, who were often resented by regular army officers, could easily have been removed from service, and elite units with special loyalty to Saddam could have been dissolved.[93] The Iraqi Army under new leadership could then have been used to help provide order rather than be left disgraced with many of its members facing destitution. The special relationship of the Iraqi Army to Iraqi society went far beyond Saddam. Even a number of anti-Saddam Iraqi exiles urged that it not be abolished.[94]

The alternative to abolishing the Army in addition to wide-ranging de-Ba'athification would have been to purge and restructure the Army. This would involve removing the political functionaries and special security forces that served throughout the military to ensure loyalty to Saddam's regime. The special security forces involved in this effort were commanded by Saddam's younger son, Qusay, and were given sweeping powers to meddle in the operations of military units despite their lack of competence in military matters. The political officials were generally detested by the professional military, who would have welcomed efforts to rid the Army of such officials.[95] Most would also have been pleased to end the long hours of ideological instruction that were supposed to support morale and readiness, but in effect detracted from unit preparation for military missions. The presence of these political units, the use of purges, and the general distrust Saddam felt for any gifted military leaders often caused many Iraqi Army officers to feel that they were victims of the regime rather than a part of it. It was, therefore, a deep shock to such individuals when the order was issued to disband them including those units that had chosen not to fight against the U.S.-led invasion.

Additionally, Saddam's primary means of control over the military was the Ba'ath Party functionaries ("commissars") noted above rather than insisting that all high-ranking officers join the Ba'ath. According to Colonel John Agoglia who served as a CENTCOM planner during this time frame:

> [I]n June, we found the personnel records of the Iraqi Army at the Ministry of Defense, and we had those computers that contained those personnel records ex-

amined by special technical experts. The special technical experts confirmed in fact that the records were authentic and not tampered with. One of the key findings of those records which was shared with [CPA Director for National Security and Defense] Mr. [Walter] Slocombe, was that in fact you did not have large-scale Ba'ath issues in the army until you got to the major general rank, and at the major general rank, 50 percent of the major generals were Ba'athists and 50 percent weren't.[96]

An important caveat is in order here, since the Iraqi Army was extremely top heavy and had more than 10,000 generals.[97] Nevertheless, the database that Colonel Agoglia mentions could have been an invaluable tool in reconstituting the Iraqi Army and then using it to help provide security for the new government. This effort would have to include extensive use of other intelligence means to confirm all aspects of the database to the greatest extent possible.

In the aftermath of CPA Orders 1 and 2, Ba'ath officials became natural allies to the angry and financially troubled ex-soldiers of the Iraqi Army after the Army was disbanded, with no effort made to recall those former soldiers who may have remained interested in serving. The ability of senior Ba'ath leaders to obtain and provide funding to the insurgency was particularly important in helping to organize it into an effective force able to include unemployed and desperate Iraqis willing to strike at U.S. forces for money. Ba'ath funding for such efforts appears to have been drawn from a variety of sources. Some Ba'ath leaders had significant reserves of cash within Iraq when the invasion occurred. This group included many mid-level Ba'athist officials as well as more senior leaders.[98] Others had access to funds in foreign banks, particularly in Syria.

The Syrians, at this time, seemed willing to turn a blind eye to many provocative Iraqi Ba'athist activities out of some ideological kinship and, more concretely, from a fear that Damascus might also be targeted for a U.S.-led regime change, unless the United States was bogged down elsewhere. Saddam loyalists who were trusted enough to have access to millions of dollars from the old regime were naturally few in number, but their ability to provide funding to unemployed ex-soldiers at the early stages of the occupation served as the lifeblood of the emerging insurgency. Later, the insurgency was to become dominated by al-Qaeda radicals, with their own funding sources from outside the country (as well as various "taxes" and asset seizures within Iraq). The senior Ba'athists able to distribute money would probably have remained committed enemies of the new Iraq under any conceivable scenario, but it would have been much more difficult for them to establish the initial insurgent networks without the large and discontented groups created by CPA Orders 1 and 2.

According to Stanford professor and former CPA senior administrator Larry Diamond, there were important warning signs that the former Iraqi officers would create severe problems if they were not given other options than simply walking away from their military careers with virtually nothing. Bremer did not seem prepared to listen or initially adjust his policies on military pensions and possible return to service by vetted individuals in the face of changing events. According to Diamond, "Bremer has set out on a decisive course — establishing the American political occupation of Iraq, dissolving the Iraqi Army and instituting a sweeping process of de-Ba'athification — and he did not want to be steered off course."[99] The refusal to adjust course may also have been reinforced by the mindset continuing to pervade the highest levels of the U.S. Government that almost all Iraqis were happy to be liberated from Saddam and that the resistance had no real social or political base to draw upon.

CPA Order 22 issued in August 2003 created the New Iraqi Army. The order forbade the inclusion of senior Ba'ath Party members in the Iraqi Army without the specific permission of the CPA. Additionally, all officers who had held the rank of colonel or above were excluded from being rehired, including those who had not resisted the U.S. invasion and were not members of the Ba'ath Party. CPA guidance suggested that all colonels and above were to be considered as committed Ba'athists, despite the bloated senior ranks of the Iraqi military, in which colonels did jobs that would be assigned to much lower-ranking officers in Western armies. The initial U.S. decision to recreate the Iraqi Army as a small force of only around 40,000 troops equipped with only light arms was an additional problem.[100] The abolition of the Ba'ath Party and the old army created a vast pool of enemies for the United States to deal with, while the decision to create only a small Iraqi military to cope with the discontent was a major problem. The most frequent explanation for this action is that U.S. leaders feared a militarized state that would threaten its neighbors and possibly mount a coup against a democratic government. The second point is particularly important since it relates back to the central U.S. fear that a new Ba'athist regime could somehow emerge through the vehicle of a military coup. Such concerns are valid, but no Iraqi government would be able to establish domestic legitimacy without being able to provide security for its population, and the Iraqi government was being set up to fail on these grounds. The U.S. delay in recognizing the dangers inherent in Iraq's lack of adequate military forces correspondingly gave the Iraqi insurgents huge advantages in establishing control over areas that would subsequently be outside the control of the central government. The U.S. leadership therefore made a deliberate decision to deny Iraq the type of force that could allow the Iraqi government to survive in the absence of U.S. forces in order to ensure that a Ba'athist coup from the military could not take place, although U.S. leaders did not seem to see this as the trade-off at the time.

The Ba'ath Party's "Political and Strategic Program," issued after Saddam's ouster, stated that its immediate priority was to "expel the occupation forces from Iraq and preserve the country as a unified homeland for all Iraqis."[101] Alienated Ba'athists did not, however, always join Ba'ath resistance organizations to fight against the Coalition and the Iraqi government. Many who wanted to fight reached out to violent Islamist groups after repenting their "sins" of supporting Saddam's secular regime.[102] These people then fought against the United States and the Iraqi government as supposed Islamic warriors. Some of this solidarity may have resulted from a decision by various Sunnis to resist the Shi'ite-dominated government by whatever means available. More pragmatically, there is also the possibility that over time the Islamist groups would be more effective than the Ba'athists in finding foreign sources of funding. Some Sunni Iraqi leaders were also forced, or at least strongly pressured, to support the fighting by al-Qaeda once it had established itself in that country. Many insurgents would again change sides when their al-Qaeda allies became too authoritarian to tolerate and when

41

the United States offered to fund the anti-al-Qaeda, "Awakening Councils."

The ability of Iranian intelligence and paramilitary organizations to function in Iraq was also aided by the portion of CPA Order 2 dissolving Iraqi intelligence organizations. This order and the de-Ba'athification order made it difficult, if not impossible, to return key personnel to intelligence duties focused on anti-Iranian counterintelligence and the containment of Iranian power. This situation is especially tricky since the intelligence organizations were important pillars of the regime, and were correspondingly riddled with potential war criminals and human rights violators. Saddam first came to power by consolidating his control over these organizations, and it appears that his youngest legitimate son, Uday, was being groomed to assume future powers as president by serving an apprenticeship within the intelligence organizations. Under a less sweeping purge, trade-offs would have had to be considered in assessing the criminality of various officials as juxtaposed against their usefulness in opposing Iran. The example of the CIA's use of former German Nazi-era general Reinhard Gehlen and his intelligence gathering organization against the Soviet Union after World War II may have served as a starting point for consideration of how this could be done.[103]

EFFORTS TO REVERSE THE EXCESSES OF DE-BA'ATHIFICATION

The idea that the United States could enter Iraq and then rapidly depart after removing much of the leadership from all major administrative structures, as well as the military as a whole, reflected an optimism that was difficult to justify. This belief was influenced by the experience of some Eastern European countries where various communist parties were removed from power without the types of problems that were to occur in Iraq.[104] Feith suggests that Iraq could have been turned over to exiles, but it was certainly not clear how these people could have established civil order or implemented a set a policies that had already been seen to create a major Sunni insurgency. In the years since the invasion, various neoconservatives have stressed that the United States should have trained a large exile army prior to invading Iraq and that by choosing not to do so helped to foreclose the option of installing exiles.[105] This approach was supposed to be based or at least inspired on the model of the French resistance in World War II and in some extreme versions may even have considered Chalabi to be a latter-day General Charles De Gaulle. Even if one accepts the logic of such an argument, the fact remains that the United States did not have such a force in place in 2002-03, and this in no way altered the ideologically based belief that the Iraq war would not require a significant occupation force to keep order after the Iraqi regime was defeated and the Iraqi Army was disbanded.

The U.S. difficulties in Iraq may also have increased due to the hostility of neighboring Arab governments and populations to policies that they viewed as anti-Sunni, such as de-Ba'athification. After the ouster of Saddam's regime, there were few credible news outlets for average Iraqis to use in an effort to understand the situation within their country. Newly emerging Iraqi newspapers were often hopelessly biased and based on a poor understanding of journalistic standards, which were unknown in Saddam's Iraq where the media's chief function was propaganda dissemination. The fledgling Iraqi television network was almost totally ignored in preference to the pan-Arab news stations such as al-Jazeera and, to a much lesser extent, al Arabibiya as well as Iran's al-Alam news broadcasts in Arabic. Some of the pan-Arab media outlets, especially al-Jazeera satellite television, were particularly hostile to de-Ba'athification Commission leader Ahmad Chalabi for a variety of reasons, not all of which involved his activities on the commission. In response, Chalabi was interviewed on al-Arabiya television where he stated that al-Jazeera was completely infiltrated by Iraqi intelligence. This statement is widely viewed as untrue, reckless, and a little desperate. This feud between Chalabi and al-Jazeera continued for some time. [106]

Moreover, as the difficulty of stabilizing Iraq became increasingly clear, Bremer became more openly critical of Chalabi's methods of conducting de-Ba'athification, which went beyond the scope of the original order. In April 2004, Bremer moved to narrow de-Ba'athification in response to the abuse of the system and to establish a more reasonable set of policies to reverse Iraq's escalating violence. He stated that the policy had been applied "unevenly and unfairly."[107] By this time, the crisis between the Sunnis and Shi'ites was exceptionally serious, and the outlines of a potential civil war were becoming increasingly clear. In response, Bremer hoped to empower a more reconciliationist Iraqi leadership that would be able to help stem the tide of insurgency. He believed that he found the right individual to lead this effort in the person of Ayad Allawi, a secular Shi'ite leader who believed in achieving national unity by reaching out to Sunni Arabs and Kurds.

Interim Iraqi Prime Minister Ayad Allawi was installed in office by the United States on June 1, 2004. On June 28, 2004, the CPA handed over formal political power to Allawi and the Iraqi Interim Government. Allawi was a longtime opponent of deep de-Ba'athification, and sought to limit the scope of the de-Ba'athification effort throughout his time in office. In a strategic vision that anticipated the Awakening Councils, he also strongly favored efforts to reconcile with Iraq insurgents and thus draw them away from hardcore Saddamists, Iraqi al-Qaeda members, and foreign terrorists. He also hoped to negotiate with Iraqi Sunnis and peel them away from their emerging alliance with foreign fighters such as al-Qaeda in Iraq leader Abu Musab al-Zarqawi. Allawi pushed forward with his efforts at reconciliation by seeking to allow Ba'athists without blood on their hands to return to state jobs. Chalabi's de-Ba'athification Commission seems to have significantly reduced its purges in response to Allawi's pressure. In justifying this policy, Allawi stated, "This country needs every single citizen" and "we will not repeat the policies of Saddam Hussein, who favored some while excluding most of the population."[108] He is also the only post-2003 Iraqi Prime Minister not to visit Iran, although he was invited to do so.[109]

Bremer presented the decision to appoint Ayad Allawi as Interim Prime Minister of Iraq as a decision made by the Iraqi Governing Council more or less on its own, which he was asked to ratify. This interpretation of events is almost universally discounted as a useful fiction designed to help Allawi by indicating that he was selected by other Iraqis and not by the U.S. leadership. Most Iraqis believe that the U.S. Government chose Allawi, and this interpretation permeates most published accounts of the event. Whatever the origins of Allawi's appointment, he nevertheless appeared to have maintained a well-reasoned and forward-looking agenda for the Iraqi future, although he also had his shortcomings on such issues as controlling corruption. Allawi met Iraqi opposition to his relaxation of de-Ba'athification from predictable sources. The leadership of SCIRI stated that "improper persons" were being given positions in the security field and this was a violation of the principles of the new Iraqi government.[110]

Feith states in his memoir that the CIA and State Department favored the Allawi appointment, but he felt that Allawi and his party were insufficiently committed to democracy. He noted that Allawi's Iraq National Accord (INA) Party had leaders who were, "supported by Sunni-controlled Arab governments [and] wanted the country's Sunni-controlled military to continue to play a key role in Iraq."[111] It is interesting that Feith was concerned not simply about the dangers presented by a Ba'athist leadership for the Iraqi Army, but he also seems to have been worried about a Sunni leadership, in general, becoming powerful within Iraq. Additionally, it is not clear why an exile group receiving support from other Arab countries allied with the United States was considered as dangerous as Shi'ite parties accepting support from Iran. Feith also notes his own serious concern about the Iranian connection to other Iraqi political parties, but does not appear to view them as any more or less troubling than Allawi's links to Arab nations such as Saudi Arabia.[112]

Prime Minister Allawi's strongly reconciliationist approach might have made progress in defeating the insurgency over time, but the decisive defeat of his party in the 2005 elections ended the chances for his approach to go forward. Sunni Arabs boycotted the election, and most Shi'ite and Kurdish voters supported parties with a clear and direct sectarian or ethnic agenda. Allawi was also undermined by reports of staggeringly high levels of corruption in his government (although this scandal did not involve him personally).[113] Allawi's term as prime minister ended on April 7, 2005, when he turned power over to Ibrahim Jaffari of the Shi'ite Islamist party, al-Dawa. Jaffari remained in power until May 2007 and was then followed by Nouri al-Maliki of the same party. Both individuals were selected through a process of internal bargaining in a Parliament dominated by Shi'ites and, to a lesser extent, Kurds. Distrust among the Shi'ite groups led to the choice of two consecutive Dawa Party prime ministers, since Dawa unlike many of the other parties has no militia, and its leaders were therefore considered safe compromise candidates.

The principles of the 2003 de-Ba'athification decree were also enshrined in the 2005 Iraqi Constitution that was largely put together by Shi'ites and Kurds (Sunni Arabs unwisely boycotted the election for the Constitutional Assembly). According to Article 131 of the Constitution, "The High Commission for De-Ba'athification shall continue its functions as an independent commission, and in coordination with the Judicial Authority and the Executive institutions within the framework of the laws regulating its functions. The Commission shall be attached to the Council of Representatives." The inclusion of this statement in the Constitution was not taken well by many Sunnis, although there were a few limited efforts to reassure them. The de-Ba'athification Commission became much more active after Allawi left office and the new

Constitution was ratified. One of their chief functions seems to have been removing people who managed to regain their jobs while Allawi was prime minister. By the summer of 2006, there was another softening of de-Ba'athification with significant numbers of people reportedly returned to the Ministries of Information, Interior, and Defense.[114] By this time, various political parties had established control over at least some important ministries and the domestic situation in Iraq appeared at its nadir. Many within the Iraqi government may have felt pressure to announce some progress on reconciliation-related issues simply to prevent the United States from giving up on Iraq.

THE "ACCOUNTABILITY AND JUSTICE ACT OF 2008"

The passing of the Accountability and Justice Act in Parliament came in early 2008 and was meant to reform the process of de-Ba'athification, as well as reverse some of its earlier excesses. The law was passed after long and tortured debate within the Iraqi Parliament in which many Shi'ite leaders made it clear that they were content with a political system that marginalized the Sunni Arab community, which they noted was only 20 percent of the Iraqi population. An earlier effort along the lines of the 2008 act has been derailed by Shi'ite opposition, including statements made by Grand Ayatollah Sistani and the three other most senior Grand Ayatollahs in Iraq.[115]

The 2008 law was enacted to respond to one of 18 benchmarks set by the U.S. Government to measure political reconciliation in Iraq. Moreover, U.S. observers often viewed it as a particularly important benchmark since it dealt with an effort to heal the

Shi'ite-Sunni divide that was poisoning Iraqi politics and undermining national reconciliation. The Iraq Parliament was correspondingly under tremendous pressure to produce some sort of a restructured and reformed de-Ba'athification law. It was also supposed to be designed to convey the message that there was now a place for the Sunni Arab elite in helping to govern Iraq. Many Ba'athists who were purged from their former positions were told that they could apply for pensions and even reinstatement in their jobs as a result of this law.

There were nevertheless problems with the new law. Many Sunnis did not view the law as liberal reform. Rather, they charged that the obtuse and ambiguous language of the law could be used to conduct further purges of ex-Ba'athists and fire soldiers and state bureaucrats who were then employed by the government. More dramatically, some former Ba'athists claimed that the law was a ploy to lure them into situations in which they could be killed.[116] Those Ba'athists in exile outside of the country have been particularly suspicious. Others assume that there is no future for them in ministries dominated by Shi'ite politicians and activists, even if their lives are not actually threatened by working there. The law therefore did not bridge differences between the Sunni and Shi'ite communities to the extent that U.S. observers had hoped it would.

Under the 2008 law, the Parliament was to appoint a new board and a new staff for the restructured commission. The individuals appointed to the board were supposed to act under amended rules and take a more reconciliationist approach to the issue of de-Ba'athification. Unfortunately, Parliament failed to meet its obligations to make these changes at the time of this writing. This failure occurred through both pro-crastination and possibly because some Members of Parliament were unprepared to approve a list of government appointments to the commission for fear that a successful effort to address this issue could be politically beneficial to Prime Minister Maliki. Under these circumstances, de-Ba'athification board chairman Ali Faisal al-Lami (then released from detention) stated in January 2010 that his board should continue to function as the new Accountability and Justice Commission (AJC) until a new board was in place. This argument was not accepted by a number of critics, and the organization continued to exist under an uncertain legal status. Although Chalabi was no longer playing a day-to-day role, it was widely believed throughout Iraq that he continued to pull most of the strings.

THE CONTINUING LEGACY OF DE-BA'ATHIFICATION IN IRAQ

A new crisis for Iraqi national unity arose on January 6, 2010, when the AJC under Chalabi and al-Lami announced the disqualification of 511 candidates in the March 7 parliamentary elections for supposed Ba'athist connections. This was done under the old quasi-legal commission's board in a sloppy and hurried manner that introduced an earthquake into the Iraqi political system. Fifty-nine of those identified for disqualification were cases of mistaken identity where individuals had names similar to those found on the commission's database. Ayad Allawi's Iraqiya Alliance suffered most under these initial rulings, with 72 of its candidates identified as disqualified. Most of the individuals identified for disqualification were from Sunni religious or secular parties, which were often supportive of Sunni Muslim political rights. Many of the most powerful Shi'ite politicians, including Muqtada al-Sadr, supported the ban. To his credit, Iraqi President Jalal Talabani strongly denounced the ban. Iraqi critics began referring to the election process as the "Iranian form of election." In Iran, a Council of Guardians evaluates the credentials of each candidate for parliament and makes a decision about their fitness to hold office as a way to constrain democracy and limit voter choice. Numerous international observers question the legitimacy of these Iranian procedures. American presidents and other political leaders have often been among those most critical of such a vetting process.

The commission's decision to disqualify such a large number of candidates in a highly opaque process also threatened to undermine the legitimacy of the election with Sunni voters. In response to complaints about the commission's actions, an appeals court initially ruled that these candidates could run for election and clear up the issue of Ba'athist affiliation later. Under reportedly heavy pressure from Maliki, the court then reversed itself on February 12, 2010, and disqualified 145 candidates.[117] If these reports are true, the AJC was enjoying political cover from the Prime Minister's office. Nevertheless, these candidates and some who were disqualified earlier were quickly replaced on their party slates so that their coalitions could continue to contest the elections with minimal disruptions. The Iraqiya political coalition was particularly hard-hit by these changes because of the disqualification of two of its leading Sunni candidates, Salah al-Mutlaq and Dhafir al-Ani. Mutlaq, who headed the National Dialogue Front of the Iraqiya coalition, was replaced by his brother on the national slate. Later, in December 2010, he became one of Iraq's two vice presidents.

As this process unfolded, the legal and ethical limbo of this entire approach to candidate disqualification was severely tainted by the fact that both Chalabi and al-Lami were running for seats in Parliament, and thereby may have hoped to benefit from the disqualification of rivals through the commission, which they dominated. The senior U.S. military leadership in Iraq was deeply disturbed by this process, and accused both Chalabi and al-Lami of being under the sway of Iran, whose leadership had a potential interest in a weak, divided Iraq that could not rise to become a regional power. In a public presentation at a Washington, DC, event, General Raymond Odierno stated that the two Iraqi politicians "are clearly influenced by Iran."[118] He added that, "We have direct intelligence that tells us that."[119] General Odierno's comments seem to raise the concern that Iran was using Chalabi as a tool to undermine Iraqi national unity. Many Iraqi leaders were more direct and strongly raised the possibility that both Chalabi and al-Lami were implementing Iraqi election procedures in coordination with Tehran for their mutual benefit.

Ironically, Chalabi and al-Lami's quasi-legal activities seem to have boosted Sunni Muslim turnout and may have caused the two leaders to lose support among Shi'ite voters. Al-Lami was not elected in the 2010 election, although Chalabi won a seat because of his party's inclusion within the Iraq National Alliance coalition list. More generally, the 2010 election did not lead to a clear outcome. Rather, strong competing political blocs emerged and were unable to put together a coalition government for 9 months. Iraqiya won a plurality of 91 seats in Parliament, but was unable to put together a coalition government. Maliki's State of Law alliance, which won 89 seats, was eventually able to do so, but only by including around 40 followers of radical anti-American cleric Muqtada al-Sadr.

A few months prior to the U.S. military withdrawal from Iraq, the Maliki government seemed intent on repeating previous mistakes by alienating Sunni Muslims. This time Maliki's actions occurred in a political environment where the United States had a decreasing level of influence. In October 2011, Iraqi authorities arrested at least 240 individuals whom they identified as former leading members of the Ba'ath Party or former important members of Saddam Hussein's army. The charges seem to imply that the arrests involved a plot by these individuals to seize power after U.S. forces depart the country.[120] Some Iraqis also appear to believe that the arrests may not have involved a specific plot as much as a general feeling that these individuals were a threat and that arresting them was a useful precaution. In defending his actions, Maliki stated that he continued to be concerned about Ba'athist "coups and conspiracies."[121] In a *Washington Post* opinion article addressed to the American public, he also asserted that, "I refute characterizations that the detentions were a sectarian action based on political motives."[122] Nevertheless, Iyad Allawi's Iraqiya political bloc has been harshly critical of the arrests and demanded the release of "all detainees held on false charges."[123]

Serious Sunni-Shi'ite differences began to escalate further, 1 day after the completion of the U.S. military withdrawal from Iraq in December 2011. At this time, Maliki moved against one of his most important Sunni rivals by issuing an arrest warrant for Vice President Tareq al-Hashemi for supporting terrorism by running a death squad. The Maliki government also arrested three of Hashemi's bodyguards and charged them with terrorism. More Sunni arrests on similar charges were expected. In describing the Prime Minister's actions, Iyad Allawi stated, "It reminds me personally of what Saddam Hussein used to do, where he would accuse his political opponents of being terrorists and conspirators."[124] Hashemi emphatically maintained his innocence, and many Sunnis assumed that the charges were politically motivated. To avoid arrest, Hashemi fled to Iraq's Kurdish north where he remained a guest of Iraqi President Jalal Talabani.[125] This move made it difficult for Maliki to arrest Hashemi since the Kurdish area has its own security forces which are not controlled by the Iraqi Prime Minister. While the Kurds and Sunni Arabs have not always been particularly close, Kurdish sensitivities were nevertheless raised by Maliki's forceful effort to consolidate power. The legacy of the Saddam Hussein regime has led many Kurds to fear a strong central government in Baghdad.

During this time frame, Maliki also sought the removal by Parliament of Deputy Prime Minister Saleh al-Mutlak of the Iraqiya bloc in response to his bitter criticism of the Prime Minister and his policies. Although serving as deputy prime minister, Mutlak had earlier been barred from standing in the March 2010 elections by the Accountability and Justice Commission.[126] In December 2011, he stated, "Maliki is worse than Saddam Hussein, because the latter was a builder, but Maliki has done absolutely nothing."[127] Additionally, while Maliki moved harshly and effectively against Sunni leaders, his government remained deeply forgiving of Shi'ite groups that had a clear history of terrorism. A variety of Shi'ite leaders are known to maintain their own militias and to have been involved with death squads and sectarian assassination. Muqtada al-Sadr serves as a particularly compelling example.

The increasing Sunni-Shi'ite differences within Iraq also paralleled the reemergence of al-Qaeda in many parts of the country. According to an August 2011 statement by Iraqi Lieutenant General Hussein Ali Kamal, Iraq's Deputy Interior Minister for Intelligence, "There was a thought that al-Qaeda had ended in Iraq. No, they regrouped and now the third generation of al-Qaeda is working actively to reorganize itself with weapons and training."[128] These words are difficult, if not impossible, to dispute. Terrorist bombings continue throughout the country, some of them with spectacular coordination and large numbers of casualties. Pilgrims visiting Shi'ite religious sites are a favored target. The government has responded to these outrages with considerable brutality against suspected Sunni terrorists to avoid charges of incompetence.

Iraq is now in a position where it will have to manage its sectarian differences without U.S. forces in that country. While the United States initiated the de-Ba'athification campaign, the Iraqi leadership twisted these policies into instruments of sectarian revenge, which its Shi'ite-dominated government is never quite willing to give up. This legacy will have to be borne by Iraqis in the absence of U.S. troops who attempted to contain sectarian differences in that country for almost 9 years. Both Iraqi Sunnis and Shi'ites (although not Kurds) celebrated that final departure of U.S. combat troops from their country, but such celebrations were held separately. Iraq will either manage its sectarian problems, or it will fail to do so. This is the choice that awaits Iraqis and will have to be faced at some point except in the event of a permanent U.S. military occupation, which is unacceptable to both countries. Any actions against the Sunnis that appear to be war crimes have infinite potential to make the situation in Iraq much worse. Iran already has a major role inside Iraq, and the Sunni Arab nations are unlikely to allow this influence to go uncontested. No Sunni nation wanted to supply arms to Iraqi insurgents and then find that American soldiers had been killed with weapons that could be traced to them. Now, in the absence of U.S. forces (except contractors), the rules have changed.

EVALUATION OF THE IRAQI DE-BA'ATHIFICATION PROGRAM

The de-Ba'athification program as it was practiced in Iraq is widely understood to have been deeply flawed in both its original conception and in the way that it was carried out. It seriously complicated all of the major challenges that the United States and its allies within Iraq faced after the ouster of Saddam Hussein's regime. These problems included the alienation of Sunni Arabs, the politicization of sectarian differences, and the rise of the Sunni insurgency. De-Ba'athification also helped to cause a number of Sunni Arab populations in neighboring countries to become more virulently opposed to the U.S. presence in Iraq, helping to undermine the U.S. presence in the Middle East and create difficulties for pro-American governments throughout the Arab World. A less dramatic approach to restructuring the Iraqi government would have substantially reduced these problems, but it would also have been seen as rendering it less likely that the United States could completely change the character of the Iraqi nation to be a close and reliable ally. Many Bush administration leaders believed that such a transformation was possible and that a new Iraq would favor permanent U.S. bases, seek U.S.

investment, support cheap oil sales, and work with U.S. allies. The decisions that were made with the idea of maximizing these goals nevertheless did very little to advance them, while instead aggravating massive problems with security and stability. A key failure here may be a lack of understanding about the limits of what can be accomplished in the aftermath of extra-regional coercive regime change in countries that are disinclined to accept foreign tutors for very long.

U.S. decisionmakers did not want to allow Ba'athist values to continue in Iraq, nor did U.S. leaders wish to allow any kind of a reformed Ba'ath to be used as a vehicle to oppose the U.S. presence and agenda in Iraq through participation in the government and administration of the country. This approach may have been aggravated by the embarrassing failure to find an Iraqi nuclear weapons program or even residual chemical and biological weapons programs. The administration, by every indication, believed such weapons existed prior to the war and, in their absence, needed to justify the intervention in other ways. The emergence of a disarmed Iraq in which some Ba'athists were still present in the government was probably not something they would view as acceptable within these parameters. Nor was a new Iraq with a traditional Arab foreign policy of opposing the West and Israel seen as a particularly compelling result for U.S. casualties and the financial cost of the war. The new Iraq was expected to look a lot more like America, or at least Turkey, than the Arab World.[129]

The worst U.S. decision made in Iraq during this time frame was not, however, a single choice. Rather, it was a combination of two decisions that reflected the desire of the United States to destroy real and imagined vestiges of the old regime at any cost. The decision by the CPA to engage in comprehensive de-Ba'athification and dissolve the Army simultaneously created the building blocks of the insurgency and provided it with the organizational capacity to create that insurgency. As noted, the Ba'ath Party did not control the military primarily through propagandizing the senior officers. Instead, it used a system of political officers and counterintelligence officers throughout the military as a way of bending the military to the regime's will. While still on balance an unwise policy, deep de-Ba'athification would seem to have precluded the need for the even worse decision of disestablishing the military. This one major advantage of deep de-Ba'athification was squandered when the second CPA order was issued. As the increasingly harsh U.S. approach unfolded, people treated like enemies correspondingly became enemies.

Attempting to understand Saddam Hussein's rule by assuming that he was a committed Ba'athist seeking to live up to Aflaq's ideals was also a serious mistake. Modern totalitarian regimes never rule in the name of naked power. They have an ideological cloak that is meant to mask the centrality of a terror state. Iraq under Saddam had a parliament, but parliamentary power was known to be a fraud. No one could have seriously held Iraq's Parliament responsible for Saddam's crimes. In the same way, the principles of Ba'athism are not necessarily offensive to all anti-Saddam Iraqis or Arabs more generally. Saddam did not build a criminal regime to serve Ba'athism. He built a Ba'athist infrastructure to support a criminal regime. The United States was correct to outlaw the Iraqi Ba'ath Party due to its hijacking by a criminal regime, but there also should have been a much greater willingness to tolerate individual noncriminal Ba'athists even if they did believe in Arab nationalism, secularism, and Arab modernization.

It might also be noted that Ba'athism is not widely viewed as the wave of the future in Middle East politics. Angry young men are seldom inspired by it, and are much more likely to join radical Islamist organizations if they seek to confront the West. In their struggle with the Israelis, Palestinian radicals are now much more likely to turn to the Islamist organization Hamas than they are to work with Fatah, the mostly secular former torchbearer of the Palestinian cause. A few Palestinians even consider Hamas and Islamic Jihad to be too tame and are seeking to affiliate with al-Qaeda-like organizations.[130] Some vigilance against the virulent alternatives to Ba'athism might have been considered. The simplistic belief that the Ba'athists were all Nazis and most other Iraqis were waiting for a Chalabi-like figure to lead them into a secular, pro-Western government created a situation in which many of the best options and opportunities for the United States were squandered.

Retrospectively, it might be noted that the problems identified with de-Ba'athificaiton in Iraq do not clearly suggest a need for changes in the structures of the military organizations involved in the war or in the ways in which they interface with civilian leaders. Many military officers were working well with former Ba'athists and saw clearly the disadvantages of a deep de-Ba'athification program. General Petraeus was doing especially well in the Mosul area in the immediate post-war time frame by implementing generous peace terms, which he eventually had to revise and make more punitive in response to orders from higher authorities. ORHA Director Garner, General Abizaid, and the senior CIA representative in Garner's staff were horrified by the implications of deep de-Ba'athification but were unable to argue against it effectively. The practical concerns of officers and intelligence professionals on the ground seem to have been overruled by civilian leaders who felt that the invasion of Iraq offered a historic opportunity to remake the Middle East in ways that benefited both the United States and the region. Once civilian authorities, including the President, had embraced this vision, the military did its best to achieve favorable results within the parameters set by civilian leaders. All leaders involved in the effort desperately wanted Iraq to be successful, but ultimately the de-Ba'athification policies proved counterproductive to achieving that goal.

PARALLELS AND DIFFERENCES BETWEEN IRAQ AND THE ARAB REVOLUTIONARY NATIONS

As noted throughout this work, some U.S. politicians feared a Saddamist restoration in Iraq to the point that they supported a policy of deep de-Ba'athification, which became a major and ongoing problem in Iraqi nation-building. Such logic was based on the Ba'ath Party's conspiratorial history and its past ability to infiltrate government and military institutions and then use them to infiltrate the government. The threat was especially serious to Bush administration leaders, since the Ba'athists in Iraq were ousted by a foreign military campaign and not a popular uprising. Consequently, the United States was placed in the position of attempting to manage what constitutional scholar Andrew Arato called, "an externally imposed revolution."[131] These U.S. policymakers believed that they had to build a radical new kind of political system in Iraq while remaining uncertain about the level of Iraqi public support for such an enterprise, which could appear to Iraqis as a foreign project designed to serve U.S. and perhaps even Israeli interests. This situation inclined some civilian U.S. leaders at the Defense Department and CPA to push for the deep de-Ba'athification that was so damaging to Iraq's national unity, causing many Sunni Muslims to believe that they were facing an externally imposed revolution that was directed primarily against them. In the Arab Spring countries, few seem to believe that regimes based on the old values and elites are likely to reestablish themselves, although equally dismal regimes could still emerge in these societies and regime "remnants" can still create difficulties. The political edge that the Arab Spring countries have is that they do not appear to have the same level of fear about the old regimes reemerging as the Bush administration leaders did about Iraq. This difference may reflect the contrast between an imposed revolution and an indigenous one.

Many Arabs involved in the 2011-12 revolutionary wave consider post-invasion Iraq to be an example of what can go wrong following the fall of a long-standing dictator. Some Arab revolutionary activists are correspondingly seeking to learn from the Iraqi experience despite the very different circumstances under which Saddam and the other Arab dictators were ousted. While many within the Arab World tended to blame the United States for all of the problems associated with de-Ba'athification, this monograph has shown that many of the worst excesses resulted from Iraqi government policies undertaken long after responsible U.S. leaders had become concerned about such activities and attempted to moderate them. The horror of Iraq in 2005-06 reminds the world of the capacity of some human beings to slaughter people who lived quietly for decades as their neighbors once the restraints of a crushing dictatorship have been removed. Revolutions by their nature are illegal, and questions of law and authority are often thrown open in eras of revolutionary transformation. The new governments established in 2011 clearly wish to avoid such a phase in their own revolutions, although many face equally daunting challenges, including the dangers of new kinds of dictatorship and civil war.

Like Iraq, some of these states, including Syria and Libya, have no democratic tradition. Others, such as Tunisia and Egypt, have had more open societies and limited power-sharing among diverse elites at earlier points in their history, although authoritarian traditions have tended to be much more prevalent, especially in recent years. Moreover, at least currently, there are no leading opposition figures with the dignity, moral authority, and heroic status of a Nelson Mandela or Vaclav Havel. Such individuals can use their standing as towering historical figures to lead an effort to build a tolerant and progressive society. Weaker politicians face more serious obstacles, no matter how well intentioned they might be.

The two countries where the lessons of de-Ba'athification may have the most relevance are probably Libya and Syria, should the regime in Syria be overthrown by the revolutionaries currently struggling against it. Both of these countries have long histories of especially intense repression and no tradition of democracy. This approach contrasts with many of the Arab monarchies that are organized along the lines of a patriarchal model. In these instances, the monarch often feels the need to show that he cares about the population and is making strong efforts to ensure their welfare. While such regimes are inherently undemocratic, they are often much less brutal than the governments of nonmonarchical dictators. Social mobilization regimes, by contrast, are much more inclined to demand the society grant its full support to the self-anointed guiding leader. Monarchs have obligations to their citizens that they usually freely acknowledge. The recently deposed dictators in Iraq and Libya needed only to implement their vision for society as they defined it, while maintaining solid control over the instruments of repression. Ba'athism in Iraq was what Saddam said it was, while Libya was supposed to be guided by Colonel Muammar Qadhafi's incoherent, "Third Universal Theory."[132] Syria is organized along similar lines as Iraq with its form of Ba'athism used to legitimize rather than guide actions undertaken by the regime. Citizens in such systems have obligations to the government, but they have no right to question the leadership or the leader's vision in any public way. The Qadhafi and Assad political systems made only cosmetic concessions to more liberal or tolerant societies. [133] Nevertheless, it remains appropriate to begin the discussion of the lessons of de-Ba'athification and the Arab Spring with the two countries where the Arab Spring began, Tunisia and Egypt. These were the first and easiest of the 2011 Arab revolutions.

Tunisia and Egypt.

The first two Arab Spring dictators overthrown in 2011 were President Zine al-Abidine Ben Ali of Tunisia and then President Hosni Mubarak of Egypt. While parallels between Saddam Hussein's Iraq and

63

these countries exist, differences vastly outnumber similarities. The Tunisian and Egyptian regimes were clearly dictatorships, but they were also dramatically less repressive than that of Saddam Hussein. Torture and violence were used against dissidents in both countries, but systematic, crushing repression on the scale of the Iraqi regime was absent. Additionally, there was not a clear ethnic-sectarian dimension to either of these regimes, as there was in Iraq, where a minority Sunni-led Arab regime brutally oppressed the large and important Kurdish and Shi'ite elements of the population, although no Sunni was ever immune from government repression either. Under normal circumstances, the interest in revenge should be milder in Tunisia and Egypt than in Iraq, and there should be no calls to oppress one element of the population on a sectarian basis as a part of that revenge. In this regard, the occasional, but harsh brutality including murder that has been unleashed against Egyptian Coptic Christians has not been the result of anti-Mubarak anger, but rather the expression of religious prejudices that a weak caretaker government has been unwilling or unable to contain fully. Thus, violent Islamic extremists seem to have taken advantage of a more permissive environment for the abuse of Coptic Christians.[134] In this instance, the Iraqi example is quite disturbing, since Iraq's Christian community was persecuted and shattered by newly empowered Islamists after Saddam was ousted in 2003.[135]

In Egypt and Tunisia, the militaries of both countries remained intact during the revolutionary process and continued to play a significant post-war role. In both countries, the military made an early decision not to support a crumbling dictatorship and to instead side with demonstrators; the military, therefore, avoided going down with the old regime. The Tunisian Army set the example by refusing to fire on anti-government demonstrators.[136] This behavior contrasted with that of the Tunisian police who were more deeply complicit with the 23-year dictatorship of the Ben Ali regime.[137] The Egyptian Army also emerged from its country's revolution completely intact, having quickly refused to back President Mubarak's efforts to retain power and being particularly unwilling to strike against the civilian population. The rapid decision by the Egyptian military leadership to support the demonstrators may have been facilitated by their strong aversion to the idea of serving under President Hosni Mubarak's son, Gamal, if he succeeded his father (as was widely expected). Gamal Mubarak had no military service, traveled in circles of extreme crony capitalist wealth, and was widely viewed as likely to rise to power without much merit through the backing of his father. Even those generals who were not adverse to a new strongman, seldom liked the idea of a "ruling family" or "republican monarchy."[138] Consequently, to the Egyptian military, the uprising was an important opportunity to avoid eventual subordination to Mubarak's widely disliked son. This coincidence of interest among opposition groups and the military allowed the regime to be deposed after only 18 days of unrest, but this victory only temporarily suppressed the profound differences between the military and the civilian opposition. Currently, the Supreme Council of the Armed Forces (SCAF), which established a caretaker government after Mubarak was ousted, is viewed with considerable distrust by many revolutionaries, political parties, and particularly the Islamists.

There was no equivalent to de-Ba'athification in either Tunisia or Egypt, although both states had dominant parties that functioned primarily to support the dictator. Tunisia's ruling party, the Constitutional Democratic Rally (RCD) Party, was forced from power in February 2011, not long after Ben Ali fell. The RCD had served as Tunisia's ruling party since that country achieved independence in 1956, and was often viewed as a path of political advancement. Party leaders attempted to save the organization and their own power base after Ben Ali fled to Saudi Arabia by formally expelling him and his closest associates from the RCD.[139] This act had no practical effect and was largely viewed as a desperate public relations stunt. Some senior politicians also quit the party during this time frame in an effort to remain in office, although these machinations usually did not save their positions. The RCD was formally dissolved in March 2011 by the post-Ben Ali leadership, and its funds were impounded. Concurrently, a number of senior party officials were arrested but always on specific charges, usually related to corruption.[140] Other government and party leaders fled into exile to avoid trial. This orderly and respectable approach to the old regime is not surprising. In January 2011, Dr. Moncef Marzouki, one of Tunisia's leading dissidents, who was soon to become the first post Ben-Ali president, commented on the RCD by stating, "We don't want any revenge, but we are fast with our principles that this horrible party does not return."[141] A variety of other Tunisian revolutionaries echoed these statements, while explicitly maintaining that they did not want to repeat the mistakes of Iraqi de-Ba'athification.[142] Their focus remained arresting those at the top of the regime, although Saudi Arabia ignored repeated requests to extradite the former Tunisian dictator. Around 40 other senior leaders are currently being prosecuted for the killing and wounding of anti-Ben Ali protestors.[143]

On October 23, 2011, competitive elections were held in Tunisia for a 217-member National Assembly to draft a new constitution. The newly legalized Ennada Party won 41 percent of the total votes, translating into 91 seats within the National Assembly.[144] This party is usually viewed as moderately Islamist, although some Tunisian secularists and others fear it could become more dogmatic if it is able to obtain and consolidate power.[145] Much of the support for Ennada appears to have been a result of the organization's unflinching opposition to the Ben Ali dictatorship, which outlawed and persecuted it for a number of years. Even some secular voters cast their ballots for this organization in the belief that an empowered Ennada is the most likely way to ensure that former Ben Ali supporters never regain power. Additionally, during the election campaign, Ennada strongly emphasized its sterling record of confronting the previous regime.[146]

The challenge in Tunisian society now seems to be between secular, European-oriented citizens and those interested in a government more closely guided by Islamic religious principles. There are parallels with Iraq's first competitive elections. Islamists did quite well in those instances, although extremists such as Muqtada al-Sadr are not as important in the Tunisian system.[147] As in Iraq, it appears that the defeat of a corrupt but secular dictatorship helped to open a serious path for Islamist political victories in at least the short term. Such victories are not inherently alarming unless the Islamists attempt to consolidate their power and remain in office through undemocratic means. Ennada's current success is a result of a "backlash election" in which its popularity directly mirrored the unpopularity of the RCD. As that party involves itself in the more mundane aspects of governance, such popularity will probably fade. Additionally, other parties can be expected to catch up with Ennada's superb campaign organization if the Tunisian system remains democratic and the new constitution reflects a basic fairness to all legal political organizations.

Egypt under Mubarak, like Tunisia, was officially a multiparty system, but election laws were manipulated and outcomes rigged to ensure that members of the President's National Democratic Party (NDP) dominated the Parliament. This party had around 3 million members in the days leading up to the revolution. In the aftermath of Mubarak's ouster, the NDP was abolished by an Egyptian court in April 2011. Its property and funds were ordered to be turned over to the Egyptian government, and its former members were prohibited from running for office in one province. While these restrictions occurred only in one province, the Egyptian judiciary did not tolerate this curtailment of civil rights. The Supreme Administrative Court overturned the prohibitions preventing these individuals from running for office.[148] This approach should be understood to be fundamentally different from de-Ba'athification, since all citizens are invited to participate in political life in the new regime. Indeed, at the time of this writing, a plausible candidate for the new presidency was Amr Moussa, Mubarak's popular one-time foreign minister, whose international contacts may be useful in restoring desperately needed foreign investment for the Egyptian economy. Additionally, some former NDP members have now re-emerged as members of various minor political parties such as the Freedom Party.[149] Nevertheless, as new elites consolidate power, they could turn more forcefully on former NDP members, and calls for banning them from standing for elections continue and could intensify over time. Even this approach would nevertheless be significantly milder than de-Ba'athification, which fired large numbers of people from state bureaucracies as well as leading politicians.

As in Tunisia, Islamists did exceptionally well in Egypt's first set of openly contested elections. The Muslim Brotherhood's newly established Freedom and Justice Party won the most seats of any political party, while the more hardline Islamist Nour (light) Party came in second in the elections for the lower house of Parliament. The Muslim Brotherhood's impressive performance is not surprising. Even while illegal, this organization had been deeply involved in charitable activities, including, in particular, providing support for the poor. The Mubarak government tolerated the Brotherhood's charitable role because it had no interest in diverting its own resources to address the problems of the poor. This background strongly parallels that of the Sadr Movement in Iraq both before and after the U.S.-led invasion. Moreover, although tolerated, the Muslim Brotherhood was illegal, and its leadership was sometimes subject to arrest and persecution.

This Islamist electoral success may pave the way for these organizations to take power, although this is not fully certain. The SCAF is still playing a significant potential role, and presidential elections may still produce a strong secular leader. Additionally, even if the Islamists are able to dominate Egyptian political institutions, they will almost certainly have to behave in a way that does not isolate Cairo from important U.S. and European sources of foreign aid, international investment, and tourism income. Any new Egyptian government that presides over an economic downward spiral, let alone a freefall, cannot be expected to last for very long. The Muslim Brotherhood seems to understand this situation and has already asserted that they will not renounce Egypt's peace treaty with Israel.[150] The leadership of the Muslim Brotherhood has also indicated that it is interested in working with secular parties.

The Egyptian Revolution therefore seems to be less comprehensive in reordering society than the process that occurred in Iraq due to the U.S.-led invasion. While the NDP has been outlawed, the SCAF remains dominated by colleagues and decades-long friends of President Mubarak. Moreover, during the Mubarak regime, the military was repeatedly scrutinized to make certain that Islamists did not infiltrate its ranks. The result of this process is a senior leadership that is deeply wary of the Muslim Brotherhood and other Islamists, such as the Salafis associated with the Nour Party. Egyptian politics correspondingly seems to be increasingly dominated by the conflict between the military leadership and the emerging Islamists with a declining economy serving as the domestic context. Secular parties are also a player in this struggle, although their influence is limited by failures in competitive elections with the Islamists. As this struggle continues, the military seems focused on maintaining its role as a powerful autonomous actor in the Egyptian political system, including control over significant economic resources that are unrelated to military functions. Under such a scenario, the military role will remain similar to its situation under Mubarak. Moreover, state television and print media tend to portray SCAF leader Field Marshal Hussein Tantawi in the same fawning light as they applied to President Mubarak during his years in power, providing something of an echo of the earlier regime.[151] Conversely, in a key difference, the nonstate media can be extremely critical of the military's actions as was seen during the February 2012 soccer riots.

Libya.

There are a number of differences between the Iraqi and Libyan situation, but events in Iraq do have limited parallels to Libya, because the legacy of long and brutal dictatorships in both countries. Fortunately, a number of Libyans appear to see Iraq as a cautionary tale for them.[152] At least some Libyans view the near civil war in Iraq as a result of a cycle of revenge and backlash between Iraq's Sunni and Shi'ite communities, which carries important lessons for them. Although Libya is not factionalized along sectarian lines such as those in Iraq, there are important regional, tribal, and some ethnic differences. Responsible Libyans are consequently concerned about maintaining national unity and avoiding internal armed conflict. They are also aware of how quickly national unity can break down following the ouster of a brutal dictator. More ominously, building a unified and functioning society in Libya will be significantly more challenging than rebuilding Tunisia or Egypt, since both of the earlier revolutions were much less violent, and both of these countries retained a functioning political, economic, and institutional infrastructure that survived the dictatorships. In the aftermath of Qadhafi's defeat and death, it is not even fully clear that Libya will be able to maintain itself as one nation. Libya only became a unified nation under its first and only king in the 1950s, after having been liberated from Italian fascism. The major regions are Cyrenaica in the east,

Tripolitania in the west, and Fezzan in the southern part of the country. Political integration of these regions occurred to some extent under the monarchy, but not under the Qadhafi regime, which sought to take advantage of regional disagreements.

Libya had no political parties under the Qadhafi regime, and there was no direct equivalent to the Ba'ath Party. There was, however, the Revolutionary Committees Movement set up by the regime to create vehicles for pro-regime activism. Like the Iraqi Ba'ath Party, these organizations are sometimes identified as important components of government, although real power has always resided with the dictator, his family, and his closest associates. Such organizations were nevertheless charged with a role in "defending the revolution," and were often used as a tool of political and ideological surveillance as well as key enablers of corruption. Under these circumstances, the National Transitional Council (NTC) decision to abolish these organizations appears wise and gives up very little administrative talent, unlike the process of de-Ba'athification. While Qadhafi was probably just as ruthless as Saddam Hussein, his regime was nowhere near as well-organized for repression as Iraq.[153] Many individuals associated with these groups have a lot to answer for, including human rights abuse and torture. The questions that remain are; how to establish a clear dividing line between the worst offenders and the others, as well as how to ensure that justice is dispensed on an individual basis and does not expand into collective punishment. The Iraq example indicates the vital role of fair judicial institutions rather than highly political commissions for such tasks. As noted earlier in this work, Ambassador Bremer has openly acknowledged his mistake in not engaging the judiciary on these kinds of issues.

Future armed conflict in Libya could occur among squabbling victors or between the new government and former supporters of the old regime, including traditionally pro-Qadhafi tribes, cities, and regions. As in Iraq, long-established rivalries and feuds are beginning to re-emerge as a side effect of the collapse of the old regime's repressive apparatus. The new Libyan leadership is aware of this problem, but has only limited tools for preventing or containing it. Building new institutions and agreeing upon the rules to prevent and regulate post-Qadhafi conflict will not be a simple or minor set of tasks. One positive factor is that during the fighting, the anti-Qadhafi leadership of the NTC was deeply concerned about maintaining international support for the anti-Qadhafi struggle, and this attitude may extend into the post-war period when the new government is seeking international support for trade and economic development. Since the overthrow of the Qadhafi regime, a variety of Libyan leaders have indicated their concern that ongoing conflict or large-scale acts of revenge would create problems for international backers and potential international investors in post-Qadhafi Libya. Unfortunately, there are a variety of incentives to seek revenge. Libyan sources maintain that around 30,000 Libyans were killed in the course of the revolution to overthrow the Qadhafi regime.[154] Such numbers are not inconceivable for the long months of bitter struggle.

A key problem is that the new government has only limited control over the erratically-trained militia forces that are nominally subordinate to them. In order to build a system based on law and order, something will have to be done to either professionalize or disarm militia forces. This is expected to remain a long-term problem, since many of these forces view maintaining their arms as an important way to ensure that they are not losers in establishing a new order. Many also believe that they have an essential role in providing local security against criminals and rivals. On a few occasions since Qadhafi's death, fighting has broken out between rival militias.[155] Establishing the rule of law will be an especially difficult challenge in Libya, where a number of different militias report to different commanders, and arrests often seem to be arbitrary.

Rebuilding a modern professional Libyan military force is therefore a serious challenge. During the dictatorship, the military was deliberately kept weak because of Qadhafi's fear that a new coup could emerge from their ranks. Such fears were well-founded. There have also been repeated reports of serious coup and assassination attempts against Qadhafi from the ranks of the military in the years prior to the revolution. More dramatically, a large-scale army mutiny took place in October 1993, with up to 2,000 troops participating in the effort to overthrow the dictator.[156] The center of the uprising was the city of Misurata where local troops nominally under government authority were not trusted to quash the uprising. The Air Force was therefore used to bomb the rebels until they surrendered. This incident did not end military discontent with the regime, and coup attempts in 1996-97 may also have involved military coordination with Qadhafi's Islamist enemies.[157] Qadhafi attempted to address the danger of a rebellious military by creating special army brigades under the authority of his sons, Khamis and Moatassim. Khamis' 32nd Brigade was responsible for the dictator's personal security and was considered his most loyal unit. Each of these units nevertheless fragmented badly in the last part of the 2011 civil war and experienced a number of desertions.[158]

Most of the prisoners from the pro-Qadhafi units, such as the Khamis Brigade, now claim that they never fired their weapons, they joined only for the money, and they were not involved in torture. Nevertheless, pro-Qadhafi troops did commit a variety of war crimes throughout the conflict. Before the imposition of a North Atlantic Treaty Organization (NATO) No-Fly Zone over Libya, Qadhafi ordered the Libyan Air Force to bomb urban areas in the hands of the uprising. Most pilots involved in the conflict followed these orders, although a few defected to Malta or Italy. A willingness to refuse unlawful orders was therefore the exception and not the rule. Another particularly ghastly set of crimes against civilians involved the regime siege of Misurata, Libya's third largest city. This siege involved regime efforts to retake the city thorough a variety of means, including the use of artillery and multiple rocket launchers to fire indiscriminately into civilian areas. These attacks included the use of cluster munitions against the civil population. Orders for such tactics are almost certain to have come from the regime's leadership. Other war crimes, including the massacre of prisoners and the use of rape as a weapon of war, have also been charged, although it is not clear where the orders for these atrocities actually originated. It therefore seems likely that many of Libya's citizens will seek justice in the aftermath of the conflict.

It is, of course, known that some anti-regime forces committed war crimes as well, but these appear to have occurred at the small unit level and were not part of any overall National Transitional Council (NTC) strategy. Senior NTC figures did not order war crimes, and, because of their limited control over the militias, probably had no real ability to halt excesses at the tactical level. Such excesses were serious but appear more limited compared to the actions of the regime, where a furious Qadhafi seemed willing to do just about anything to crush the people he called "rats." Libyan authorities are unlikely to pursue excesses by their own militia troops at this time due to an urgent concern to limit future fissures within the ranks of the revolutionary movement. At this time, it may be more important for them to begin to professionalize the individuals who are expected to remain in the new Libyan Army so that they behave with restraint and military discipline in the face of future challenges and particularly domestic unrest that may continue to plague Libya. Some crimes committed on the rebel side may nevertheless be too serious to overlook indefinitely, and it may be less divisive to address them rather than ignore them. The unsolved murder of NTC General Abdul Fatah Younes on July 28, 2011, may be an example of such a crime. This assassination is widely believed to have been a result of internal differences in the anti-Qadhafi forces, possible because of Younes' background as a former Qadhafi interior minister.[159]

In addition to former soldiers, there are questions of the future of pro-Qadhafi tribesmen in the new Libya. Libya is a highly tribalized society with around 140 tribes and clans, of which 20 to 30 are considered large and important. Qadhafi's own tribe, the Qadadfa, is sufficiently small and weak, that the dictator had no choice except to reach out to individuals from other tribal units to help establish a base of power. Unsurprisingly, members of pro-Qadhafi tribes (such as the Magarha) have dominated the Qadhafi regime's security forces, and it may be difficult to fully disentangle individual actions from those encouraged and abetted by tribal leaders and authority figures. This situation could invite the prospect of collective punishment from a vindictive successor regime. Some of the most important tribes, such as the Werfella, had combatants on both sides of the struggle to overthrow Qadhafi. This situation helps to mitigate the danger of collective punishment to some extent.

Beyond the dangers of unrestrained revenge, many of the new Libyan leaders are also concerned about the potential problems of building a new government with effective and legitimate institutions. Colonel Qadhafi had some unusual ideas about government, and his divisive and bizarre approaches to governance left little foundation on which to build. Qadhafi was openly contemptuous of political institutions and claimed to have developed a new form of government based on revolutionary democracy expressed at the grassroots level. As seen with a variety of oil-rich countries, Colonel Qadhafi organized a strong public sector in Libya which he used to increase popular dependency on the government and to support claims of limited unemployment.

While the Libyan government has a number of serious problems, there are also some positive factors for the country's future. One of the most important of these factors is the country's economic potential. Like Iraq, Libya is an important oil-producing state, but it also has only about a fifth of the Iraqi population. Moreover, it now appears that Qadhafi diverted huge sums of money to various secret bank accounts and investments, which are now available to the current Libyan leadership. One estimate suggests that there may be as much as $200 billion in such accounts.[160] While economic potential did not save Iraq from large-scale sectarian conflict, the possibility of a dramatically higher standard of living for virtually all Libyans would seem to be a positive factor in addressing problems such as youth unemployment, which can increase the potential for unrest. The experience of both Iraqi de-Ba'athification and the disbanding of the Iraqi Army illustrated the severe dangers of spikes in youth unemployment in post-revolutionary systems. The Iraq experience suggests that the sooner the government is able to use its considerable resources to create reconstruction jobs, the safer Libya will be from a downward spiral into instability.

Syria.

Unlike Egypt and Tunisia, the ouster of the Syrian regime may take years of struggle, if it occurs at all. At the time of this writing, more than 5,500 Syrian civilians had been killed by the military and security forces as part of this conflict, and the rate of civilian deaths may yet increase rather than decline. Syria is ruled by a Ba'athist dictatorship, which has a number of similarities with Saddam Hussein's Iraq. Current President Bashar al-Assad rose to become the leader of Syria in 2000 following the death of his father. Syria is, for all practical purposes, a one-party state with its own branch of the Ba'ath Party providing the ideological façade for a system of government designed to protect the privileged position of those currently in power.[161] Syria, also like Iraq, is a patchwork of different sectarian groups, and Syria's ongoing revolutionary struggle has profoundly sectarian overtones. Since 1970, Syria has been led by presidents from the Assad family, members of the Alawite sect, which is generally considered to be a branch of Shi'ite Islam. The Alawites of Syria, at 10 percent of the population, are a much smaller portion of the Syria's total population than the Arab Sunnis of Iraq who comprise 20 percent of the population of their country. Most of the most important members of the government, military, and Ba'ath Party are from the Alawite sect or other minority communities allied with the Alawites. Sunni Muslims constitute around 70-75 percent of the population, whereas Christian and other minorities comprise the remaining portion.

Throughout much of Syrian history, Alawites were an ill-treated, impoverished religious minority who were seldom able to obtain anything more than the worst employment that the society had to offer. Their fortunes improved somewhat when opportunities to serve in the French colonial army became available after France occupied Syria as a League of Nation's mandate following World War I. The legacy of being near the bottom of Syria's socioeconomic ladder weighs heavily on many current members of the Alawite community as they contemplate their future under either a Sunni-dominated democracy or a Sunni-led dictatorship. If post-Assad Syria was to be dominated by Islamists, their views of the Alawites could be even further poisoned by claims their sect is heretical. Such beliefs are widespread among Sunni Islamist hardliners. Additionally, many Alawites undoubtedly fear Sunni revenge for 40 years of brutality and misrule under the Assads. The bloody conflict that has raged over the last year has also added horrendous new grievances to the already long list of injustices for which the Alawites may be held accountable. Saudi writer Essam al-Zamel has acidly summed up this situation with almost literal gallows humor by stating, "The greater the tyrant's resistance to his people, the worse his punishment. It seems that Bashar [Assad] will be crucified to death in the center of Damascus."[162]

While many Alawite leaders and even ordinary Alawite citizens fear that they will be punished should the regime be deposed, they may not be alone in such fears. Many non-Alawite minorities, especially the large Christian community, are concerned that the Syrian revolution may create a Sunni-dominated Muslim government that will severely curtail their rights.[163] Unsurprisingly, many members of these groups show some reluctance to support the anti-Assad uprising, although they also fear that any highly visible support for the government could cause them to experience more problems in the aftermath of a successful revolution against Assad. Christians looking at the fate of their co-religionists in post-Saddam Iraq cannot help being disturbed about their potential fate in the aftermath of successful revolution. Additionally, the rapid rise of Islamists in Tunisia and Egypt following the ouster of the dictatorships raises concerns that a similar result may occur if there is a successful revolution in Syria.

It has already been noted that the Arab Ba'ath movement began in Syria and spread to Iraq from there. In Syria, as in Saddam' Hussein's Iraq, the Ba'ath Party is primarily a policy implementation tool and an instrument for mobilizing the society to support the government. While the party is a bulwark of the regime, it does not have much input to the president or other key decisionmakers. Real power is concentrated in the Assad inner circle and the top ranks of the security forces, which are dominated by Alawites with strong links to the Assad family. Interestingly, a significant number of lower-ranking Ba'ath Party members resigned in protest from the organization at the early stages of the uprising, indicating some disagreement within the party.[164] It is likely that many of these dissenting individuals are Sunni Muslims who joined the party to improve their ability to obtain jobs, money, and privileges. Their resignations appear to have been only a minor inconvenience for the regime as it shifted its strategy for controlling the uprising to one dominated by force and brutality.

Throughout the over 40 years of the Assads' de-facto dynasty, the Syrian government has made an extraordinary effort to immunize the regime from coups or uprisings. This approach has involved a relentless effort to neutralize the Army's capability to engage in anti-regime action of any kind. Bashar's younger brother, Maher Assad, commands the Syrian Army's elite Republican Guard Division and the equally well-equipped Fourth Armored Division, both of which are composed predominantly of Alawites and are completely loyal to the regime.[165] Non-elite units are led by loyalist officers throughout their chain of command, and military personnel are monitored carefully by the security services. The independence shown by the Egyptian Army during the Tahrir Square demonstrations is unthinkable in Syria.

Assuming that they avoid summary execution in the aftermath of being overthrown, Assad and his key supporters will almost certainly be tried for mass murder, and they know this. With the possible exception of Iran, there seems to be relatively few places where they can flee. Additionally, Bashar understands that his safety and that of his associates depends upon retaining an unreformed police state, which he views as the only guarantee of Alawite privileges and safety. Qadhafi is reported to have asked his executioners,

"What did I ever do to you" in his last hour of life, apparently stunned at the depth of hatred against him. Bashar is under no such illusions. He is aware of his crimes and aware that only a strong dictatorship can prevent him from sharing Qadhafi's fate.

The Syrian regime will probably never be overthrown by nonviolent protesters, whom they are willing to kill in whatever numbers they need to in order to remain in power. Since these tactics are increasingly viewed as ineffective, the opposition seems more willing to consider armed opposition. If Assad is to be overthrown, this will have to be done by armed struggle, and the effort to oust the dictator may well continue to evolve into an increasingly bitter civil war. The other side of this approach is that the Syrian regime will use armed opposition to justify increasing its own level of repression, which is already at extremely high levels. All of these factors indicate that the Syrian government will use all of the repression of which it is capable rather than liberalize the regime in a way that fundamentally threatens the power of the current elites. Many reports cited by Western news agencies have accused Syrian military units of indiscriminate shelling of civilian areas thought to be opposition strongholds.[166] The use of such tactics was later confirmed by Arab League monitors, whom the Syrian regime accepted into their country to buy time before its case was sent to the UN Security Council. These monitors have now departed Syria.

The Syrian military has held together extremely well throughout much of the uprising, although there are increasing reports of defections.[167] Some of these defectors have fought against pro-regime units, but they have neither the organizational infrastructure nor the logistics and supply network necessary to maintain themselves as a conventional military force.

Various spokesmen for the defectors call these forces the Free Syrian Army (FSA). While some units of the FSA have been allowed to seek sanctuary on Turkish soil, there is no indication that Ankara is involved in any effort to arm, equip, or train these units.[168] Moreover, at the time of this writing, FSA forces in Turkey did not seem to comprise more than a few hundred individuals. Nevertheless, as the carnage continues, it is likely that Sunni conscripts will feel increasing psychological pressure to defect. The conscripts make up the majority of forces in the non-elite military units.

In light of the above considerations, any program of de-Ba'athification in Syria could be especially brutal because of the ever-growing list of crimes the regime has committed against the Syrian people to remain in power. It has been noted that some Iraqis spoke of de-Ba'athification as de-Sunnization, and the prospect for all Syrian Alawites to be viewed as regime supporters suggests that de-Ba'athification in Syria would take on a sectarian character as well. While most Alawites sympathize with the Assads, not all Alawites have committed crimes to support them. The prospect of a post-revolutionary Alawite bloodbath is therefore something that all responsible friends of a new Syrian government would have to guard against. It is not, however, clear that neighboring Arab governments will push hard in that direction, since all of them, except Iraq, have Sunni leadership. Many Lebanese fear that sectarian hatred in Syria could spill over into their own country, but Lebanon has very little ability to moderate actions within Syria. Perhaps the best hope is that a post-revolutionary government will need a great deal of aid for reconstruction and development, and any anti-Alawite bloodbath would inevitably cause the United States and Europe to suspend such aid and call upon Arab states to do so as well.

Yemen.

At this time, only one additional Arab leader has been ousted as part of the Arab Spring upheavals, former President Ali Abdullah Saleh of Yemen. There are probably relatively few lessons that Yemen can draw from Iraq's experience with de-Ba'athification. Yemen has never maintained a strong centralized government such as could be found in Iraq under Saddam. President Saleh ruled by political opportunism, manipulation, and bribery as much as by repression. One of Kuwait's post-1991 foreign ministers once characterized him as a dictator like Saddam Hussein, but this is not true. Saleh never had the apparatus of repression that Saddam maintained, and many of his leading officers appear almost as opportunistic as the former president. In situations such as this, Yemeni officers have often had the political space to consider their own interests in deciding if they will continue to support Saleh.

Yemen is a multiparty system, and while former President Saleh's political party, the General Peoples Congress, may not be abolished, it will almost certainly be weakened. The powerful Islamist party, Islah, is its most likely successor. Such an ascendancy would hardly be good news for the United States, which had designated the Islah party leader as a terrorist supporter. Nevertheless, no new leader in Yemen is likely to establish a strong central government. The powerful Yemeni tribes and the military will probably continue to dominate the political system. General Ali Moshen, a former Saleh lieutenant who defected to the rebels along with the forces under his command, may emerge as an especially important post-Saleh leader.

Indeed, Saleh has largely viewed the entire process as an effort by Moshen and his supporters to replace him.

CONCLUSION

The United States had a level of involvement in the Iraq de-Ba'athification program in 2003 that will not be duplicated in efforts to support contemporary Iraq or to construct new political systems in the Arab Spring states considered in this work. The United States will therefore be in a position to grant advice and support to friendly states, but it will not be able to play a major role in organizing new political systems as it once sought to do in Iraq. Yet, the experiences with de-Ba'athification are probably too valuable to be completely dismissed and provide a number of important examples of the difficulties inherent in establishing a post-dictatorial government. In everything it does regarding both contemporary Iraq and the Arab Spring nations, Washington will therefore have to draw from relevant experience, while remaining aware of its more limited influence. Such influence must be used wisely. In Libya, this approach seems to offer some promise. The U.S. decision to work behind the scenes of the NATO intervention into Libya rather than play a leading role has limited U.S. responsibility for the aftermath in that country. While the United States provided essential support to the Libyan operation, the decision to play a limited role in the actual fighting seems to have helped Washington avoid General Colin Powell's famous, "you break it, you own it," pottery barn rule. This situation suggests that the United States can offer advice and support when this seems prudent, while remaining in the background in other cases when that seems wise. Within these guidelines, the following recommendations are offered for addressing concerns about the future of Iraq and the Arab Spring with the lessons of de-Ba'athification as a consideration. Some of these recommendations may also be relevant for non-Arab countries, including Iran, if their populations rise against oppressive regimes in Arab Spring-type revolts. Regional experts and policymakers might wish to consider such parallels on a case-by-case basis.

1. The United States must continue to do whatever it can to support a process of national conciliation in Iraq. In order to do this, U.S. leaders must remain attuned to problems in Iraq and elsewhere that may push the country toward state failure. The Bush administration often seemed to view democracy as a wholly positive transformative system without fully understanding the ways in which it can go wrong in deeply polarized and sectarian societies. As noted, these mistakes were eventually understood by many U.S. leaders over time, but, by then, the dynamics of sectarian conflict were especially difficult to contain and roll back. The United States must nevertheless continue to express its disapproval for politicized and reckless de-Ba'athification procedures in Iraq. Washington must also stress that political institutions used as instruments of sectarian oppression always hold the potential to incite civil war in societies that have not been totally crushed by their governments, one of the worst outcomes imaginable.

2. Officers and senior non-commissioned officers (NCOs) of the U.S. Army must realize that they may often have unique opportunities and unique credibility to offer advice on the lessons of Iraq, including the problem of de-Ba'athification, to their counterparts in some of the Arab Spring nations. The U.S. Army has a long history of cooperating with some of the Arab Spring militaries and has a particularly strong relationship with the Egyptian military. These bonds of trust and teamwork can be used to convey a variety of messages beyond exclusively military issues. Additionally, many U.S. Army officers gained a great deal of experience in Iraq from which they can draw upon to highlight the ways in which revolutionary change can go wrong.

3. The United States will have to use the lessons learned about Iraqi de-Ba'athification to assess ways in which Arab Spring countries may be failing. U.S. leaders must also consider ways to advise or otherwise help struggling governments. One of Iraq's key problems was the rapid development of the view among some Iraqis that democracy is a winner-take-all form of government. The activities of the de-Ba'athification Commission often helped to reinforce that view among both Shi'ites and Sunnis. All Arab Spring governments will need to take care that new post-authoritarian institutions do not reflect a similar winner-take-all mentality among leaders, sects, tribes, political groups, or regions. The United States can draw upon its experiences in 2003 Iraq to make this message known to new governments, but unlike Iraq, the United States is not in a situation where it must take ownership of the Arab Spring. This means that U.S. leaders will have to have the dexterity to recognize when their advice is helpful and welcome and when it may be a source of resentment and conflict.

4. The United States needs to help strengthen and support judiciary institutions in the Arab Spring countries and strongly emphasize the need to resolve issues of guilt or innocence within a judiciary framework rather than a commission composed of politicians or any similar organization. The United

States should laud any efforts in these countries to advance the concepts of rule of law and support the activities of UN specialized agencies and other nongovernmental organizations (NGOs) seeking to provide aid to judicial bodies in the post-revolutionary states. It has already been noted that Iraq's de-Ba'athification Commission was administered by politicians, and that these politicians were running for office against people who they disqualified for participation in the election. In no part of the planet can this be considered fair. Seeking to honestly establish the guilt of those accused of political crimes as well as their punishment is best left to judges if a fair court system can be established and maintained. Eligibility for particular individuals to run for office should likewise be addressed by unbiased judicial institutions.

5. The United States needs to be careful to avoid the appearance of publicly picking out and then lobbying for favorite leaders in the new Arab Spring governments, as it did with Ahmad Chalabi in Iraq. If these countries are lucky, they may find a dignified and fair-minded national leader, although it would be a mistake for outside forces to attempt to generate one. The U.S. experience with Chalabi in Iraq might be particularly instructive here. U.S. leaders should not underestimate the distrust that many Arab populations feel for the United States. U.S. support for a leader with strong connections in Washington is not always well received by a populist electorate. No nations are so close that their publics want another state to choose their leadership for them. Additionally, problems have already resulted when Qatar chose to support some Libyan politicians and factions over others in their aid programs. Qatar was the strongest Arab backer of the Libyan revolution, and Doha has a lot more latitude to get away with this type of approach than does the United States. In spite of this situation, there are already numerous complaints that Qatar is interfering in Libyan internal affairs when it does so.[169]

6. **In Iraq, the United States learned that free elections produced a great deal of hope but also a variety of problems, and U.S. leaders must consider the lessons of this experience as they formulate policy involving the Arab Spring states.** Competitive elections are clearly a positive development, but they do not always indicate an increase in stability or tolerance within a society. It is therefore important that elections are viewed as the beginning of a process of democratization and not as the culmination of such a process. Protection of minority rights and the importance of peaceful transitions of power from one elected government to another are also key pillars.

7. **The United States needs to indicate a willingness to work with Islamist governments so long as those governments remain democratic, respect human rights, respect minority rights, and show some level of cooperation on key regional problems such as counterterrorism and nuclear nonproliferation.** In Egypt, the United States needs to be willing to engage the Muslim Brotherhood and communicate the need for that organization to continue a variety of important Egyptian policies, including respect for democratic procedures, willingness to work with the military, and respect of the Egyptian-Israeli peace treaty. The United States has a reputation with some Middle Eastern citizens, including many Iraqis, of favoring democracy only when regional democracy produces pro-American candidates. A U.S. unwillingness to judge any Egyptian government by its actions can only feed that narrative, and U.S. leaders need to be

open to the possibility of partnership with a democratic Muslim Brotherhood-led government. Conversely, any new Egyptian leadership should be made aware of policy changes and red lines that might seriously disrupt normal relations. U.S. policymakers and military officials dealing with foreign militaries will have to remain nimble in making judgments about the differences among Islamic groups and the degree to which U.S. cooperation with new leaders is wise or even possible.

8. The U.S. Army and other services also need to work closely with the Egyptian military through a variety of programs already in place, if this is at all possible. The U.S. civilian and military leaderships should do everything possible to resolve whatever problems it might have with the Egyptian leadership, while leaving such programs in place. Such an effort must be based on an understanding that the military exists to serve democracy and must avoid policies that violate human rights. Nevertheless, another reason to cultivate the Egyptian military is that it is in a key position to keep politicians honest. A military that views itself as above politics will resist governmental efforts to act in extra-constitutional ways and should be particularly unwilling to serve as the repressive arm of any government that seeks to retain power by overriding democratic procedures. Any effort by the Islamist parties to purge the military for political reasons is correspondingly a cause for serious concern.

9. The United States must be exceptionally wary about involving itself in the Syrian revolution against the Assad regime, in the full understanding that Syria is just as complicated as Iraq and not every Middle Eastern problem has an American solution. It is not yet clear how the Syrian revolution will play out, but it seems highly unlikely that NATO will adopt similar policies to those in Libya. The words of journalist Michael Hirsh, "What happens in Libya, stays in Libya," correctly suggest that a unique set of factors enabled international action against the Qadhafi regime, and that this set of factors is unlikely to be duplicated elsewhere in the Arab World.[170] Syria, in contrast, would present a hornets' nest of problems comparable in intensity to those the United States encountered in Iraq. Even without foreign intervention, it seems unlikely that the Assad regime will be able to crush the opposition by force, which remains its goal at this time. It also seems unlikely that the regime will offer more than simply cosmetic efforts at power-sharing. If the regime is overthrown, the United States must seek to work with post-Assad revolutionaries, but ultimately may be viewed with distrust in the Arab World for any effort to involve itself in combat. Like the Iraqis, the Syrians have enduring decades of propaganda about U.S. conspiracies to control the Middle East.

10. The U.S. leadership must also understand that, to an even greater extent than the Iraqis, Syrian citizens may be susceptible to anti-Western conspiracy theories and distrustful of U.S. intensions. The close U.S. friendship with Israel is especially likely to create Syrian distrust about any U.S. agenda for their country. Despite some occasional Iraqi participation in the conflict with Israel, including the 1973 Arab-Israeli War and the 1991 Scud missile strikes, Iraq is usually a peripheral player in the Arab-Israeli conflict, while Syria is at the core of the conflict. The Iraqis viewed the U.S. presence in their country with steadily increasing criticism, with Washington receiving very little credit as a liberator, due to a local belief that the United States invaded their country to advance its own agenda for obtaining cheap oil and establishing military bases that could be used to dominate the region. In Syria, suspicions of an alternative U.S. agenda favorable to Israel could only be stronger. This situation is not an insurmountable problem, but it may also indicate the need for the United States to allow other friendly nations to play a major role in helping to resolve problems in Syria should Assad be overthrown.

11. The United States must maintain an ongoing dialogue with its closest regional allies, including Israel, Jordan, and Saudi Arabia, about the changes that are occurring in the Arab World, and Washington would do well to consider their views in the formulation of policy. This type of behavior was not always apparent in Iraq on the issue of de-Ba'athification when some allies such as Jordan and Saudi Arabia considered the United States to be dismissive of their views in favor of its own poorly informed assumptions. These assumptions included the belief described by Professor Fukiyama that the default position for a defeated dictatorship is always a liberal democracy. The Jordanians and the Saudis had been living in that region long enough to know better. The Jordanians had even seen a branch of their own ruling family ousted by a military coup in Iraq and then watched a succession of new and more brutal dictatorships emerge in that country culminating in the rule of Saddam Hussein. While the United States may ultimately disagree with these countries, their views have earned serious consideration.

12. The United States must understand that the rise of Islamists in the Arab Spring countries is not an aberration and is likely to continue to occur in additional cases, although it is uncertain that Islamists will dominate any of these countries in the

long term so long as democratic institutions persist. The U.S. leadership will need to understand that in the aftermath of a dictatorship, those individuals and organizations that the dictator most violently oppressed often emerge with vastly enhanced prestige. In some cases, they may emerge as a new set of elites. In many countries, these people will be Islamists. All of the regimes that have been overthrown as part of the Arab Spring were basically secular just as the Saddam Hussein regime was predominantly secular, although greater religious expression was allowed in the regime's last decade as a safety valve to relieve popular misery and discontent. In Tunisia, Egypt, and Libya, Islamists poised the main opposition to the regimes and were consequently subjected to the greatest degree of repression. Unsurprisingly, in all of these countries, the status of Islamists has been enhanced by the degree of opposition that they presented to the former regimes. Moreover, the Islamists, by virtue of their years of opposition and persecution, are sometimes seen as presenting the clearest break from the old regime. Some Islamic parties also have a network of mosques and Islamic charities that can be called upon to aid in the election of Islamic candidates and help to fill a vacuum created by the collapse of other institutions.

13. The United States must seek to support economic stability in the Arab Spring countries so long as they remain friendly and democratic, while reminding Arab leaders of the economic problems associated with failed efforts at national unity in their countries. In Iraq, the difficulties of the Sunni Arabs led to an insurgency that routinely attacked Iraq's economic infrastructure, including the oil industry. Building democratic, accountable, and transparent governments will not be easy for any of the Arab Spring governments. Libya will be harder than Egypt or Tunisia, and all countries need to understand the importance of avoiding a downward spiral.

14. The U.S. Army will have to be aware that it may be asked to play a limited role in rebuilding the Libyan military. The United States will also have to deal with the Libyan government on a variety of issues, such as shoulder-fired anti-aircraft weapons accountability, and has a stake in the new government's success. This situation suggests that various forms of military expertise and training may be provided to a responsible Libyan government at some future point. Such efforts will undoubtedly complement efforts by other countries to help Libya, including its major trading partners in Europe and the Arab League. It may also be possible, although not likely, that Libya may have the building blocks of an insurgency. Pro-regime holdouts conducted impressive defense of Sirte and Bani Walid for some time after the rest of the country was liberated.

15. The United States might wish to offer advanced military training and education to Libyan officers that includes Western concepts of civil-military relations. Such training is already provided to officers of other Arab Spring militaries. Additionally, army officers who defected from the Libyan army and fought for the rebels have a clear expectation that they will have a role in the future of Libyan national security. These concerns need to be channeled in ways that allow democratic processes and institution building to move forward. If the Syrian government is overthrown, the United States may wish to consider ways to reach out to help professionalize the military and keep it out of politics. U.S.-Syrian relations may nevertheless be complicated by issues involving Israel and the Palestinians in ways that will not occur with Libya.

ENDNOTES

1. Francis Fukuyama, *America at the Crossroads, Democracy, Power, and the Neoconservative Legacy*, New Haven, CT, and London, UK: Yale University Press, 2006, p. 116.

2. King Abdullah II of Jordan, *Our Last Best Chance: The Pursuit of Peace in a Time of Peril*, New York: Viking, 2011, p. 226.

3. As quoted in Tom Heneghan, "Libyans Stress Harmony to Avoid Iraq-Style Chaos," *Reuters*, September 4, 2011.

4. On the use of this phrase, see Douglas J. Feith, *War and Decision*, New York: HarperCollins Publishers, 2008, p. 202.

5. Saddam Hussein's regime later claimed without evidence that Aflaq had made a deathbed conversion to Islam in 1989, at a time when his propaganda machine was attempting to respond to Iranian charges that his regime was "Godless." See Amatzia Baram, *Culture, History and Ideology in the Formation of Ba'athist Iraq, 1968-89*, New York: St. Martin's Press, 1991.

6. The Syrian and Iraqi branches of the Ba'ath displayed a long-standing inability to work with each other and a continuing struggle for leadership of the Ba'athist movement. Brief periods of partial reconciliation were usually followed by long periods of hostility and conflict.

7. Baram, p. 13.

8. Hanna Batatu, *The Old Social Classes and the Revolutionary Movements of Iraq*, Princeton, NJ: Princeton University Press, 1978, p. 1010.

9. Efraim Karsh and Inari Rautsi, *Saddam Hussein: A Political Biography*, New York: The Free Press, 1991, p. 15.

10. *The Next Civil War? Sectarianism and Civil Conflict*, Brussels, Belgium: International Crisis Group, February 2006, p. 7.

11. This was not always the case due to the vicious family politics practices among Saddam's relatives. In one instance in 1995, Saddam's two sons-in-law defected to Jordan after they became concerned that Saddam's son, Uday, might kill them either in a fit of rage or as part of an organized plan. When they foolishly returned to Iraq after being unable to establish themselves as viable opposition leaders, Saddam had them killed. See Said K. Aburish, *Saddam Hussein*, New York: Bloombury, 2000, pp. 337-339.

12. On the literacy programs, see Majid Khadduri, *Socialist Iraq: A Study in Iraqi Politics since 1968*, Washington DC: The Middle East Institute, 1978, p. 140.

13. Baram, p. 137.

14. On this political culture, see Wendell Steavenson, *The Weight of a Mustard Seed: The Intimate Story of An Iraqi General and his Family during Thirty Years of Tyranny*, New York: HarperCollins Publishers, 2009.

15. Karsh and Rautsi, pp. 112-119.

16. In keeping with the nature of the political system, Aziz thanked the leader slavishly for concerns about his health.

17. This type of punishment occurred in the case of a senior general in 1990. He appears to have been executed after the amputation. See Neil MacFarquhar, "Saddam believed he would rule forever," *International Herald Tribune*, December 31, 2006, Internet.

18. Gordon W. Rudd, *Reconstructing Iraq: Regime Change, Jay Garner, and the ORHA Story*, Lawrence, KS: Kansas University Press, 2011, pp. 146-147, 249.

19. Linda Robinson, *Tell Me How this Ends: General David Petraeus and the Search for a Way out of Iraq*, New York: Public Affairs Press, 2008, pp. 70-72.

20. Bremer, pp. 39-40.

21. See, for example, Feith, *War and Decision*, p. 240; and Don Eberly, *Liberate and Leave: Fatal Flaws in the Early Strategy for Postwar Iraq*, Minneapolis, MN: Zenith Press, 2009, p. 27.

22. Ahmed S. Hashim, *Insurgency and Counter-insurgency in Iraq*, Ithaca, NY: Cornell University Press, 2006, p. 15.

23. Andrew J. Bacevich, *The Limits of Power: The End of American Exceptionalism*, New York: Henry Holt and Company, 2008, p. 165.

24. Hashim, chap. 5.

25. Feith, p. 202.

26. On the concept of "de-Arabization," see Hashim, p. 385.

27. Bob Woodward, *The War Within*, New York: Simon and Schuster, 2008, pp. 120-121.

28. Transcript of Interview with Lieutenant General Jay Garner, "The Lost Year in Iraq," *PBS.org*, posted October 17, 2006.

29. *Ibid.*; Rudd, p. 313.

30. Colonel John Agoglia, as quoted in Charles H. Ferguson, *No End in Sight*, New York: Public Affairs Books, 2008, p. 155.

31. Public Broadcasting Corporation Transcript, *"Frontline: The Lost Year in Iraq,"* October 17, 2006.

32. Vice President Cheney was an exceptionally strong supporter of deep de-Ba'athification. See Graham, p. 462.

33. Bremer interview as cited in Public Broadcasting Corporation Transcript, *Frontline: The Lost Year in Iraq*, October 17, 2006.

34. Bob Woodward, *State of Denial: Bush at War Part III*, New York: Simon & Schuster, 2006, pp. 196-197. The author has also heard a similar account from an officer who worked with General Abizaid during this time frame. This officer also maintained that no one who knew General Abizaid at this time could fail to understand his opposition to harsh and sweeping de-Ba'athification.

35. Draper interview with President Bush as cited in Robert Draper, *Dead Certain: The Presidency of George W. Bush*, New York: Simon & Schuster, Inc. 2007, p. 211.

36. L. Paul Bremer III, "How I Didn't Dismantle Iraq's Army," *New York Times*, September 6, 2007.

37. Bremer, p. 21.

38. Chap. 2 of Bremer's book is entitled "Taking Charge." See Bremer, p. 23.

39. Rudd, pp. 307-308.

40. Packer, p. 240; Rudd, pp. 310-311.

41. Rudd, p. 327.

42. *Ibid*, p. 132.

43. Allawi, p. 149.

44. *Ibid.*, p. 150.

45. For an exploration of these issues, see Christian Caryl, "Iraq's Young Blood," *Newsweek*, January 22, 2007, pp. 25-28.

46. Packer, p. 192.

47. On nominal Ba'athists, see Rudd, p. 270.

48. Lieutenant General Ricardo S. Sanchez, *Wiser in Battle, A Soldier's Story*, New York: HarperCollins Publishers, 2008, p. 186.

49. According to a 2008 article co-authored by Bremer, the CPA sought to reverse deep de-Ba'athification. But by the time it did so, "the CPA's authority was waning, and the dominant [Shi'ite] and Kurdish political factions in Baghdad had little or no interest in allowing even innocent Ba'athists back into public office." See L. Paul Bremer, James Dobbins, and David Gompert, "Early Days in Iraq: Decisions of the CPA," *Survival*, August/September 2008, p. 31.

50. Feith, p. 431.

51. Sanchez, p. 184.

52. Bremer, Dobbins, and Gompert, p. 30.

53. Allawi, p. 147.

54. Hashim, pp. 280-283. The author has met with numerous Iraqis and other Arabs who have strongly asserted this view and none who disagree with it.

55. Diamond, pp. 192-193.

56. Allawi, p. 151.

57. Bremer, p. 341.

58. "Interview with L. Paul Bremer" in "Key Controversies and Missteps of the Postwar Period," as cited by PBS in website supporting documents for *Frontline: The Lost Year in Iraq*, October 17, 2006.

59. Packer, p. 168.

60. Bremer maintains that he asked the IGC to take over de-Ba'athification, and they chose Chalabi to lead this effort without his input or advice. This seems surprising since Chalabi clearly had strong allies among the leading Pentagon civilians pushing for de-Ba'athification and since Chalabi's base of power was then in Washington and not in Iraq. See interview with L. Paul Bremer III," Public Broadcast Service," *Frontline: The Lost Year in Iraq: Documents, Key Controversies and Missteps of the Postwar Period*, 2007, available from *www.pbs.org/wgbh/pages/frontline/yearin Iraq/analysis/fuel.html*.

61. Ahmad Chalabi, "Iraq for the Iraqis," *Wall Street Journal*, February 19, 2003.

62. Packer, p. 202.

63. For some of Chalabi's highly positive statements on Israel and the potential for Iraq-Israeli relations, see Tom Brokaw, "A Conversation with Ahmad Chalabi," Council on Foreign Relations Event, June 10, 2003, available from *www.cfr.org/iraq/conversation-ahmad-chalabi/p6044*.

64. "Chalabi's Defeat Presents Quandary," *MSNBC.com*, December 22, 2005, Internet.

65. Don Eberly, *Liberate and Leave: Fatal Flaws in the Early Strategy for Postwar Iraq*, Minneapolis, MN: Zenith Press, 2009, p. 159.

66. Packer, p. 336.

67. Hashim, p. 91.

68. "Iran's 'Invisible man'," *The Middle East*, August/September 2008, p. 31.

69. "Iraq: Your Man or His?" *Economist*, October 7, 2006, p. 56.

70. On the concept of a democratic ornament, see Heribert Adam, *Modernizing Racial Domination; South Africa's Political Dynamics*, Berkeley, CA: University of California Press, 1972.

71. *The Next Iraqi War*, pp. 9-10.

72. Associated Press, "Saadoun Hammadi, 77, Premier and Top Aide to Saddam Hussein, Dies," *New York Times*, March 18, 2007.

73. Christine Moss Helms, *Iraq Eastern Flank of the Arab World*, Washington DC: Brookings, 1984, p. 91.

74. Helms, p. 106.

75. Dilip Hiro, *Neighbors, Not Friends: Iraq and Iran After the Gulf War*, London, UK, and New York: Routledge, 2001, pp. 50-51; Charles Tripp, *A History of Iraq*, New York: Cambridge University Press, 2000, p. 258.

76. Doha Al-Jazirah Satellite Channel Television, "US Troops Ignored Tribe's Request for Release of Hammadi," July 5, 2003, as reported by Foreign Broadcast Information Service (FBIS), now the Open Source Center, July 5, 2003.

77. *The Next Iraqi War*, p. 10.

78. The exception to this principle included ex-Ba'athists such as Ayad Allawi, who fled into exile and then became active in anti-Saddam opposition movements.

79. *Corruption Perceptions Index 2011*, Berlin, Germany: Transparency International Secretariat, 2011. Note Iraq is currently tied with Haiti for the rank of 175 out of 183 governments for its perceived levels of public sector corruption, with one being best and 183 being worst.

80. Borzou Dargahi and Said Rifai, "In policy reversal, Chalabi reaches out to Baathists," *Los Angeles Times*, January 18, 2007.

81. Damien Cave, "Iraqis Answer Global Critics by Tackling Troubling Issues," *New York Times*, January 18, 2007.

82. Rajiv Chandrasekaran, "On Iraq, U.S. Turns to Onetime Dissenters," *Washington Post*, January 14, 2007.

83. "U.S Arrests Key Iraq Official for Suspected Ties to Militia," *Los Angeles Times*, August 29, 2008.

84. Benedetta Berti, "Salafi-jihadi Activism in Gaza: Mapping the Threat," *West Point Center for Combating Terrorism Sentinel*, May 2010, pp. 5-9.

85. Al-Sharqiyah Television (Dubai), August 29, 2008, as recorded by BBC Worldwide Monitoring.

86. As cited in Robert H. Reid, "Senior Iraqi official suspected of Militia Links," *Associated Press Online*, August 28, 2008.

87. Rod Nordland, "U.S. Will Release More Members of an Iraqi Militia," *New York Times*, August 17, 2009.

88. "Iraqi Official Who Ousted Baathists Is Slain," *Washington Post*, May 27, 2011.

89. The author has held discussions on this topic with a senior officer involved in this effort. Also see Bradley Graham, *By His Own Rules: The Ambitions, Successes and Ultimate Failures of Donald Rumsfeld*, New York: Public Affairs, 2009, p. 402.

90. Packer, p. 302.

91. Fukuyama, pp. 115-116.

92. Packer, p. 97.

93. Hashim, pp. 5-6.

94. The author of this report is a co-author (with Conrad Crane) of a pre-war report urging that the United States purge, but not abolish, the Iraqi Army if it chose to invade Iraq. Much of this same case was made by at least some well-known Iraqi exiles, such as my friend, Dr. Mustafa Alani. When in 2006, I travelled to Dubai, I again met Dr. Alani, who asked, "Andy, why didn't anybody listen about the Iraqi Army?" I had no answer. See Conrad C. Crane, W. Andrew Terrill, *Reconstructing Iraq: Insights, Challenges, and Missions for Military Forces in a Post-Conflict Scenario*, Carlisle, PA: Strategic Studies Institute, U.S. Army War College, February 2003, pp. 32-33.

95. Hasim, pp. 5-8.

96. As quoted in Ferguson, *No End in Sight*, p. 176.

97. James Fallows, "Why Iraq Has No Army," *The Atlantic Monthly*, December 2005, p. 64.

98. Hashim, p. 29.

99. Larry Diamond, *Squandered Victory*, New York: Times Books, 2005, p. 54.

100. Thom Shanker, "U.S. is Speeding up Plan for Creating a New Iraqi Army," *New York Times*, September 18, 2003.

101. Hashim, p. 121.

102. *Ibid.*, p. 117.

103. On the Galen unit, which became the nucleus for West German intelligence, see Leonard Mosley, Dulles, NY: Dial Press, 1978, pp. 236-238, 240-242. For a somewhat more skeptical view, see Tim Weiner, *Legacy of Ashes: The History of the CIA*, New York: Doubleday, 2007 pp. 42-43.

104. "Deputy Secretary of Defense Wolfowitz interview with Lucian Mandruta," Pro TV [Romania], U.S. Department of Defense Press Release, Internet; and Michael Dobbs, "For Wolfowitz, A Vision May Be Realized," *Washington Post*, April 7, 2003, p. A17.

105. "Talk with former CIA Director James Woolsey," *CNN.com*, October 30, 2003, Internet.

106. Hugh Miles, *Al-Jazeera: The Inside Story of the Arab News Channel that is Challenging the West*, New York: Grove Press, 2005, pp. 289-294.

107. "Help from the Baathists," *Christian Science Monitor*, May 6, 2004.

108. As cited in Zaki Chehab, *Inside the Resistance: The Iraqi Insurgency and the Future of the Middle East*, New York: Nation Books, 2005.

109. Mahjoob Zweiri, "Arab-Iranian Relations," in Anoushiravan Ehteshami and Mahjoob Zweiri, eds., *Iran's Foreign Policy: From Khatami to Ahmadinejad*, Reading, Bershire, UK: Ithaca Press, 2008, p. 118.

110. Hashim, p. 56.

111. Feith, p. 240.

112. "Ahmadinejad, Saudi King hold more phone talks: IRNA," Agence France Presse (AFP) October 21, 2010.

113. *Corruption Perceptions Index 2011*, Berlin, Germany: Transparency International Secretariat, 2011.

114. "Inside Iraq: Ex-Ba'athists get their jobs back," *Reuters*, August 7, 2006.

115. "Sistani opposes Bill on the Baathists," *Irish Times*, April 3, 2007.

116. "A Hint of Political Compromise at last," *Economist*, January 19, 2008, p. 48.

117. Ernesto Londono and Leila Fadel, "Chalabi is back, and the U.S. isn't happy," *Washington Post,* February 27, 2010.

118. Thom Shanker, "General Say 2 Iraq Politicians have Ties to Iran," *New York Times*, February 17, 2010.

119. *Ibid.*

120. Ahmed Rasheed and Suadad al-Salhy, "Iraq rounds up Baathists ahead of U.S. pullout," *Reuters.com*, October 25, 2011.

121. Nouri al-Maliki, "Building a Stable Iraq," *Washington Post*, December 5, 2011.

122. *Ibid.*

123. "Allawi says Iraq headed for 'sectarian autocracy'," *Kuwait Times*, December 29, 2011.

124. "Iraqi Sunni leaders denounce PM Maliki," *Khaleej Times*, December 21, 2011.

125. "Sunni lawmakers keep up Iraqi parliament boycott," *Jordan Times*, January 4, 2012.

126. "Iraq PM moves to oust deputy as US forces leave," *Jordan Times*, December 19, 2011.

127. *Ibid.*

128. "Qaeda, Shia militias pose threat to Iraq," *Gulf Times*, August 29, 2011.

129. Turkey was sometimes cited as a favored model for Iraq in the 2004-05 time frame.

130. Benedatta Berti, "Salafi-Jihadi Activism in Gaza: Mapping the Threat," West Point Center for Combating Terrorism, *Sentinel*, May 2010, pp. 5-9.

131. Arato's concept is quite complex, and it is worth referring to his study for a fuller explanation. See Andrew Arato, *Constitution Making Under Occupation: The Politics of Imposed Revolution in Iraq*, New York: Columbia University Press, 2009, Chap. 1.

132. On the "Third Universal Theory," see Ronald Bruce St. John, *Libya: From Colony to Independence*, Oxford, UK: Oneworld, 2008, pp. 157-59.

133. For example, see Alexandra Zavis and Alexandra Sandels, "Syria holds local elections as deadly clashes reportedly continue," *Los Angeles Times*, December 13, 2011.

134. Yasmine Saleh, "Egypt Christians in two minds over Islamist Gains," *Jordan Times*, December 9, 2011.

135. Peter Durkovic, "Iraq's Christians, Lebanon's Shame," *The Daily Star*, November 4, 2011; "Iraq's dwindling Christian community faces new uncertainty," *Los Angeles Times*, December 17, 2011.

136. "Tunisia Army Pivotal to Ben Ali Ousting-Reports," *Jordan Times*, January 18, 2011. Note that Admiral Jacques Lanxade, a former French Chief of Staff and later Ambassador to Tunisia, stated that the Army decision not to fire on demonstrators was key to the collapse of the dictatorship.

137. Alexis Arieff, *Political Transition in Tunisia*, Washington, DC: Congressional Research Service, September 20, 2011, p. 10.

138. Discussions held with senior Egyptian military officers.

139. "Tunisia coalition hits trouble on day two," *Jordan Times*, January 19, 2011.

140. *Ibid.* p. 3.

141. "Tunisia ministers quit government as protests resume," BBC News, January 18, 2011.

142. Kemel Riahi, "A Night in Tunisia," *New York Times*, January 18, 2011.

143. "Tunisia says Saudi silent on requests to extradite ex-leader," AFP, January 4, 2012.

144. For a complete breakdown of the election results, see Erika Atzori, "Tunisia leads the way," *The Middle East*, December 2011, p. 19.

145. The party's name is French for "Renaissance," so, ironically, an Arabic translation would render it as the Ba'ath Party. Nevertheless, the name is used in a completely different context, and Ennahda has nothing to do with Saddam's Ba'ath Party.

146. "Islamists to the fore," *Economist*, October 29, 2011.

147. Bouazza Ben Bouazza, "Tunisia's Islamist party slams anti-Semitic chants," Associated Press, January 9, 2012.

148. "Mubarak party members allowed to run in Egypt vote," *Jordan Times*, November 15, 2011; Leila Fadel, "Egyptians Fear Return of Mubarak Allies," *Washington Post*, November 17, 2011.

149. Abdelrahman Youssef, "Mubarak-era figures recycle careers in rural Egypt," *Reuters*, January 9, 2012.

150. "Brotherhood's 'laxity' on Israel treaty stuns Hoss," *The Daily Star*, January 14, 2012.

151. Jeffrey Fleishman and Amro Hassan, "Egypt Military Giving Signs of Not Wanting to Relinquish Power," *Los Angeles Times*, November 3, 2011.

152. Tom Heneghan, "Libyans Stress Harmony to Avoid Iraq-Style Chaos," *Reuters*, September 4, 2011.

153. This is not to say that repression was not severe. For a moving novel on this subject, see Hisham Matar, *In the Country of Men*, New York: Dial Press, 2008.

154. "Libyan Estmate: At least 30,000 died in the war," Associated Press, September 8, 2011.

155. "Rival Libyan militias clash near army base," *Kuwait Times*, November 14, 2011.

156. Ronald Bruce St. John, *Libya: From Colony to Independence*, Oxford, UK: Oneworld, 2008, p. 223.

157. *Ibid.*

158. Thomas Erdbrink, "Vaunted Khamis Brigade Fails to Offer Much Resistance to Libyan Rebels," *Washington Post*, August 21, 2011.

159. Rami al-Shaheibi and Hadeel al-Shalchi, "Libyan Rebels Try to Impose Control," *TIME*, August 10, 2011.

160. Paul Richter, "As Libya takes Stock, Moammar Kadafi's Hidden Riches Astound," *Los Angeles Times*, October 22, 2011.

161. In Syria, some smaller political parties have been allowed to operate as Ba'athist allies in a cosmetic effort to make the regime appear more democratic. These parties might be best viewed as democratic ornaments which have no political role other than to suggest broad support for the regime.

162. As quoted in Liz Sly and Leila Fadel, "In wake of Libyan uprising, attention turns to Yemen, Syria," *Washington Post*, October 21, 2011.

163. "Syrian Stalemate," *The Middle East*, November 2011, p. 18.

164. Liz Sly, "Report Hint at Cracks in Syria Regime," *Washington Post*, April 28, 2011; Elizabeth A. Kennedy and Diaa Hadid, "Syrian Army Units Turn on Each other Amid Crackdown," *Boston Globe*, April 29, 2011.

165. Kathierine Zoepf and Anthony Shadid, "Syrian Leader's Brother Seen as Enforcer of Crackdown," *New York Times*, June 7, 2011.

166. "Defiant Assad Praises Troops after Deadly Syria Crackdown," *Jordan Times*, August 2, 2011.

167. Khaled Yacoub Oweis, "Anti-Assad fighters defy odds in Syrian town," *Jordan Times*, September 29, 2011.

168. Liam Stack, "In Slap at Syria, Turkey Shelters Anti-Assad Fighters," *New York Times*, October 27, 2011.

169. Sam Dagher, "Tiny Kingdom's Huge Role in Libya Draws Concern," *Wall Street Journal*, October 17, 2011.

170. Michael Hirsh, "What Happens in Libya Stays in Libya," *National Journal*, October 20, 2011.